your loved ones are

always

with you

CONNECTING WITH THE OTHER SIDE

zena

THOUGHT CATALOG Books

THOUGHTCATALOG.COM

THOUGHT CATALOG Books

Copyright © 2024 Zena.

All rights reserved. No part of this book may be reproduced or transmitted in any form or any means, electronic or mechanical, without prior written consent and permission from Thought Catalog.

Published by Thought Catalog Books, an imprint of Thought Catalog, a digital magazine owned and operated by The Thought & Expression Co. Inc., an independent media organization founded in 2010 and based in the United States of America. For stocking inquiries, contact stockists@shopcatalog.com.

Produced by Chris Lavergne and Noelle Beams
Art direction and design by KJ Parish
Creative editorial direction by Brianna Wiest
Circulation management by Isidoros Karamitopoulos

thoughtcatalog.com | shopcatalog.com

First Edition, Limited Edition Print
Printed in the United States of America

ISBN 978-1-949759-99-0

FOREWORD 7

CHAPTER 1
Death Unveiled — 11

CHAPTER 2
The Transition Phase—Departing the Physical Realm — 15

CHAPTER 3
Understanding Earthbound Versus Ascended Spirits — 21

CHAPTER 4
Embracing the Eternal Connection — 27

CHAPTER 5
Transcending Tragedy:

A Journey Beyond Untimely, Tragic, and Violent Deaths — 31

- *My Daughter's Six-Lane Highway* — 35
- *Fatal McDonald's Run* — 41
- *Black Ice, Not Speed* — 43
- *A 12-Year-Old's Final Act* — 45
- *Always a Nurse* — 48
- *Speed was a Factor* — 49
- *Left for Dead* — 51
- *All Together* — 53
- *Wrong Place Wrong Time* — 54

CHAPTER 6
Messages of Love Know No Boundaries — 55

- *Funny Grandma Lost Her Brain* — 57
- *Secret Sauce Grandfather* — 59
- *Happy Birthday Grandson* — 61
- *2 Slices of Pecan Pie, Please* — 62
- *Pepsi with a Side of Red Meat* — 63
- *Wrangler Shirt Pillow of Love* — 64
- *Two Peas in a Pod* — 65
- *Trickster Best Friend* — 67
- *Cheese Doodle Hands* — 69
- *Orange-Filled Milk Chocolate* — 70
- *Mints On the Bill* — 71
- *Mom's 7-Year Battle* — 73
- *Rosary in My Hands* — 75
- *The Kugel Grandmother* — 77

CHAPTER 7
Messages of Healing and Closure 79

   Hidden Truth 82
   Blanket of Flowers 84
   27 Shots, But Over the First 85
   All Together Now 87
   Mom Has Her Shoes 89
   Just a Country Boy 91
   Canceled Wedding 93
   Squishmallows, Squishmallows 94
   Watching Over My Girls 95
   Don't Cry Over Spilled Ashes 96

CHAPTER 8
Messages of Guidance and Protection 97

   Small Flower Assault 99
   Stop the Salt 101
   Heather Receives Nana's Warning 103
   I'm Still Here 104

CHAPTER 9
Children's Connections Across the Veil 107

   A Child Lost at Five 109
   A Voice for Mia 111
   Forever 16 Months Old 112
   Trickster Forever 113
   Squeezy Hugs for Everyone 115
   No More Squishy Face 117
   Chasing Butterflies 119

CHAPTER 10
The Eternal Journey of Unborn Souls 121

   Message From a Lost Daughter 125

CHAPTER 11
The Journey of Our Departed Pets 127

   Ozzy Bear 130
   It's My Tongue, Mommy 133
   Saint Bernard Protection 137
   Hush Puppy Nacho 141

CHAPTER 12
Barriers to Connection Across the Veil 145

CHAPTER 13
Spirit Guides and Guardians: Nurturing Souls Beyond Death 149

To my beloved Asia, who ascended during the writing of this book...

Thank you for returning in spirit to ensure I kept writing to help others know that connection is infinite.

foreword

IN THE VAST EXPERIENCES of human existence, few concepts provoke as much contemplation and curiosity as death. It is a subject that transcends cultural boundaries and penetrates the very core of our being. When we ponder the fate of the human spirit, we embark on a journey that takes us beyond the confines of our physical existence and into the realm of the unknown.

Through the ages, one theme has remained constant: the inevitability of death. From the moment we draw our first breath, we begin a journey destined to end in the embrace of mortality. Death, the great equalizer, spares no one, transcending boundaries of age, wealth, and status. It is a profound and mysterious phenomenon, shrouded in both fear and fascination, for it marks the ultimate passage from this earthly realm to whatever lies beyond.

Many of us have grappled with the concept of death and its implications for the human spirit. Countless beliefs and philosophical systems have emerged, each attempting to answer the profound questions that arise when we contemplate what awaits us on the other side.

These questions lie at the heart of our existential curiosity, urging us to seek meaning and purpose amidst the transient nature of our lives.

Longing for answers, we continue to search for understanding by confronting the central questions: What happens to the spirit when we die? Does it transcend to another realm, reunite with a divine source, or simply dissolve into the cosmic fabric of the universe?

As we search for answers to what happens to the spirit in the afterlife, it is essential to approach the mystery of death with an open mind and a willingness to embrace the ambiguity that surrounds it. The quest for answers may lead you down winding paths, challenging your preconceptions and evoking powerful emotions along the way.

It is crucial to acknowledge that you are now venturing into the realm of faith, hidden in the mystical veil that separates the living from the dead. However, because death is an integral part of the human experience, as we explore its nature, it will compel you to not only reflect on what happens to you when you die, but you may also find yourself unraveling deep-seated beliefs and questioning the actions you take in life.

Throughout this book, I will strive to bring a sense of clarity to the mysteries that lie beyond the threshold of death and are revealed to me through my experiences as a Clairsentient, understanding that the journey is as much about the questions we ask as it is about the answers we uncover. For now, let us embrace this spiritual voyage together, facing the uncertainty and curiosity that drives each of us to discover the truth about the afterlife.

We will dive deeply into the richness of human beliefs, examining the concept of the afterlife by exploring the mystical realms beyond death's veil. From uncovering universal truths to sharing my mediumship connections, I will shed light on the fate of the spirit. It is my hope that our journey into the unknown transforms your understanding of life and death, brings a sense of comfort and closure, and the transcendence of your soul.

CHAPTER 1

Death Unveiled

HUMANITY'S QUEST FOR KNOWLEDGE has always been driven by the desire to unravel the mysteries of existence. We have made significant progress in understanding the physical world, mapping the cosmos, and deciphering the complex workings of our own bodies. Yet, when it comes to the nature and fate of the spirit, we encounter blocks from our consciousness.

One of the greatest challenges in comprehending the afterlife is our limited perspective as mortal beings. Our insights are bound by the constraints of time and space, and we are confined to the physical realm. The nature of the spirit, free from these limitations, eludes our understanding. We are left to contemplate its essence based on fragments of personal experiences, testimonies, and the teachings of various traditions.

Despite the information we have gathered from these sources, the afterlife remains an enigma. This enigma encourages us to explore the deeper questions of our existence. We seek the personal meaning of our own spiritual journeys and harbor the wish to reconnect to those who have passed before us.

Throughout history, countless beliefs and theories have emerged to explain the afterlife. Some envision a heaven or paradise where souls find eternal peace and joy. Others propose reincarnation, suggesting that the spirit engages on a cyclical journey, experiencing different lives and lessons. Then there are those who perceive the afterlife as a realm of spirits, coexisting with the physical world but remaining invisible to our mortal senses.

In the face of these diverse beliefs, it becomes evident that the afterlife is a deeply personal and subjective concept. It reflects our individual beliefs, experiences, and cultural backgrounds rather than a singular truth.

Still, we can find shared solace and inspiration in the human experience of struggling with the mysteries that lie beyond our comprehension. It is in this shared exploration that we can discover common threads—universal truths that transcend cultural and religious boundaries.

The mysteries of the afterlife ask us to expand our horizons and engage in a lifelong journey of self-discovery. It is this journey that invites us to ponder the nature of our existence and the potential transcendence of our individual spirits.

However, as we explore the mysteries of what happens to the spirit when we die, we must first turn our attention to the awe-inspiring concept of the collective consciousness. This concept suggests that our individual consciousness is not isolated but interconnected with the consciousness of all living beings. It implies that our experiences, thoughts, and actions have a ripple effect, shaping the evolution of consciousness both in this lifetime and beyond.

The idea of the collective consciousness is not a new one. Many ancient spiritual traditions and mystical teachings have touched upon this interconnectedness. However, it is only in recent times that science and spirituality have started to converge, shedding light on this profound phenomenon.

When we depart from our physical bodies, we transcend the limitations of the material world and enter a realm where the collective consciousness becomes more apparent. Our individual experiences merge and intermingle with the experiences of countless other souls.

In this spiritual journey after death, the collective consciousness acts as a conduit for growth and evolution. It quickly becomes apparent that our personal growth and understanding are not only for our benefit but for the benefit of the entire collective. Every insight gained, every lesson learned, and every act of love and compassion becomes a stepping stone toward the evolution of the collective consciousness. However, it is only when we take hold of the present moment here on Earth to embrace love, compassion, and connection with others that we cultivate these qualities ourselves to carry forward into what lies beyond.

As we venture deeper into the secrets of death, it carries with it a sense of wonder for the unknown. This is where mediumship holds a key for many. These connections have captivated the human imagination for centuries, offering tantalizing glimpses into the enigmatic realm behind the veil. These encounters offer a snapshot into what lies beyond life.

The remarkable narratives I share throughout this book, from my live-streamed spirit connections over the social media platform TikTok to my private appointments, not only provide a look into the realm beyond our physical existence, but they also offer healing, intriguing clues about the spirit, vivid connections with those left behind, and insights for all of us to what awaits us after death. Those who have experienced these connections describe them as a life-altering event, transforming their perspectives on life, death, and spirituality.

At this point, it is important to note that the afterlife is subjective and unique to each individual. The experiences and perceptions I described are based on my first-hand accounts of benevolent beings and departed souls I have had the pleasure of communicating with throughout my life journey.

CHAPTER 2

The Transition Phase—Departing the Physical Realm

AS LIFE-THREATENING SITUATIONS intensify, individuals find themselves at the threshold between life and death. It is at this critical intersection, where the ethereal realm begins that many of our crossed-over loved ones have shared their experiences and this intriguing phenomenon.

In this liminal space where the boundaries between the physical and spiritual realms blur, a wide range of extraordinary events have been reported to occur during mediumship connections. Departed loved ones often speak of encounters with beloved family members, a radiant light of unconditional love, and interactions with divine beings.

With that said, the most common occurrence described by departed loved ones during these connections is the sensation of leaving their physical bodies, often hovering above the scene, observing their own resuscitation efforts, witnessing events from a new vantage point, and recalling the injuries or pains they felt. For many who have crossed over, they shared these last moments of physical existence as evidence of their presence to the loved ones they left behind, knowing how meaningful these moments are to the living.

However, for the ascending spirit, those last moments quickly give way to the significant insights uncovered during their next phase–the final life review. Many of those who have crossed over have described undergoing this comprehensive life review as a panoramic replay of their entire existence, with sensations from their past rushing through their consciousness in an instant.

To truly comprehend the meaning behind this phenomenon, we must first understand the authentic nature of our spirit. Throughout our lives, our spirits reside within the confines of the human body, tethered to the material world by the bonds of existence. But when death occurs, the spirit is liberated from its earthly vessel, and the shackles of physicality no longer confine its essence.

As our spirit prepares to cross over into the realm of the afterlife, it encounters a timeless and infinite dimension that transcends the limitations of linear time. In this extraordinary state, our spirit revisits the pivotal moments and significant events of its earthly journey. During the life review, the spirit is not merely a passive spectator but an active participant reliving the emotions, lessons, and connections forged during its mortal existence. It is at this moment that the spirit chooses to hold onto the emotions and events or to let them go.

This life-review phenomenon can be likened to a cinematic montage, an awe-inspiring tapestry that weaves together the moments that defined our existence. It is an interactive exploration of our choices, actions, and their consequences. Each scene is accompanied by a deep understanding of the ripple effects our lives have had on others and the interconnectedness of all souls. In this ethereal space, we witness our lives from multiple perspectives, empathizing with those we encountered while living and experiencing the impact of our deeds upon their lives.

This soulful reflection is not intended to be a judgmental process but rather a healing one. It serves as a catalyst for spiritual growth, fostering empathy, forgiveness, and compassion for ourselves and others. Through this introspection, we attain a deeper understanding of our soul's challenges, the patterns we were meant to navigate, and the purpose of our existence.

This spiritual growth leads to vibrational changes that permit ascension to our highest being, merging our essence with the collective wisdom and knowledge of countless other souls. The culmination of these experiences enables the spirit to transcend past personal life limitations and continue to evolve.

Once the life review is completed, a powerful shift occurs. The departing soul enters a liberation unlike any other. During this transition, they often experience a mix of emotions ranging from disbelief and sadness to relief and even joy. At this juncture, many spirits desire an opportunity to comfort those left behind, yearning to ease their grief and assure them they are still present in their lives.

Emotions experienced during this phase can be diverse and intense. There may be a sincere sense of relief from physical pain or suffering. Simultaneously, there can be a sense of loss or nostalgia for the physical life and loved ones left behind. The spirit may also feel a mixture of curiosity and awe as it embarks on this uncharted journey, venturing into the realms beyond what it knows.

As the spirit gradually moves further away from its physical being, many are enveloped in a state of tranquility. The noise and chaos of the physical realm fade into the background and are replaced by a peaceful stillness. This peacefulness allows the spirit to encounter other entities and beings. These encounters can take various forms, depending on the beliefs and expectations of the individual. Some experience a deepening connection to deceased loved ones, spirit guides, or divine beings who offer guidance, support, and reassurance. These interactions can be deeply comforting, providing a sense of familiarity and love amidst the unfamiliarity of the transition.

Perceptions of time and space also undergo a remarkable transformation during the transition phase. The spirit finds itself existing in a realm where conventional notions of time cease to hold meaning. Past, present, and future blend together in a continuum, allowing for a holistic understanding of the interconnectedness of all experiences. Space becomes fluid, and the spirit begins to move effortlessly through different dimensions and realms, exploring the vastness of existence.

While the exact nature of the afterlife remains an enigma, the phenomenon of the life review and the transition phase offers us a glimpse into the potential workings of the spiritual realm. It reminds us that our existence is not confined to the physical plane alone but extends far beyond the boundaries of our mortal comprehension. This introspective assessment becomes a poignant reminder that our actions and intentions matter. Every choice we make, every interaction we have, becomes a brushstroke on the canvas of eternity, shaping the destiny of our spirit and influencing the collective consciousness.

CHAPTER 3

Understanding Earthbound Versus Ascended Spirits

AS WE EXPLORE THE contrasting experiences of earthbound spirits versus ascended spirits, we shed light on the choices and consequences that shape the afterlife of each spirit as they cross over the veil.

When a person passes away, in some instances, their spirit may not immediately transition to the next plane of existence. These spirits are known as earthbound spirits, tethered to the physical realm by emotional attachments, unresolved issues, or a reluctance to let go.

As we think of earthbound spirits, we envision trapped souls who remain attached to the earthly plane after death. While these spirits may be bound by unresolved emotions, unfulfilled desires, or deep attachments to people, places, or material possessions—they are not trapped. Rather than crossing over to ascend to a higher realm, they choose to remain entwined with the world they once knew.

Earthbound souls are those who find themselves in limbo between the physical world they have left behind and the spiritual realms that await them. Their refusal to let go of their negative emotions, be it anger, fear, regret, or unresolved attachments, keeps them tethered to the earthly plane. Unfortunately, these souls may wander without direction, haunted by their unfulfilled desires, or even linger near loved ones with whom they are unwilling to part.

For these souls, the transition phase can be a perplexing experience. They resist the pull of the spiritual realms, feeling drawn back to the familiarity of their previous life. Their attachment to earthly existence becomes a barrier to growth and ascension, keeping them in a state of stagnation. They often struggle with a sense of longing and frustration at what they left behind and are unable to move forward.

It is important to remember that earthbound is not a judgment or punishment but rather a personal choice. Each soul has its own unique circumstances and lessons to learn. For some, the attachment to negative emotions may be deeply ingrained, requiring time and assistance to overcome. These spirits often remain near their former homes, loved ones, or locations that hold significant meaning for them. They may attempt to communicate with the living, seeking closure or resolution for unfinished business. Earthbound spirits are bound by their own attachments and often require healing or forgiveness to release themselves from their self-imposed connection.

While earthbound spirits may find themselves tethered in their attachments, there is hope for their liberation. With time, understanding, and the help of loved ones left behind, angels, spiritual guides, and divine guidance, these spirits can find resolution and release. They can ultimately ascend to higher realms, reuniting with departed loved ones and merging with the universal consciousness.

Various spiritual practices, such as mediumship and energy healing, can also help bring closure and aid in the process of releasing the earthly binds. These specialties allow for communication, healing, and resolution, enabling the spirit to move forward on its spiritual journey.

Ascended spirits, on the other hand, represent those who have successfully transitioned to higher realms of existence. These souls have embraced the transformative power of death and have let go of earthly attachments. Through a process of spiritual growth and self-realization, they have risen above the limitations of the physical plane, expanding their consciousness and understanding of their new limitless existence.

These souls are not bound by time, space, or physical constraints. They reside in realms of pure energy, where love, wisdom, and harmony prevail. These spirits have embraced their eternal nature, gaining insights from higher dimensions.

They diverge significantly from earthbound spirits due to their choice to detach from the physical world. These souls undergo a metamorphosis, shedding their earthly identity to emerge as beings of pure energy and consciousness. Once their transformation is complete, their existence is characterized by peace and a deep connection to the divine.

The contrast between earthbound and ascended spirits highlights the importance of cultivating awareness and consciousness during our physical life existence. The path a spirit takes after death, whether towards becoming an earthbound spirit or ascending to higher realms, is influenced by various factors. The nature of a person's life, the choices they made, and the lessons they learned all play a role in shaping their spiritual journey after death. Moreover, individual belief systems and personal experiences can influence how one perceives the transition from the physical to the spiritual realm.

It is our life choices, beliefs, and attachments that shape our postmortem experiences. Earthbound spirits serve as a reminder of the unfinished business and unresolved emotions that can bind the soul to earth, while ascended spirits immediately embody the infinite potential for growth, expansion, and enlightenment.

With that said, in the realm of spirits, whether they are earthbound or ascended, both hold a relationship to the earthly plane. Earthbound spirits often interact with their loved ones, seeking opportunities for growth, healing, and closure. Ascended spirits act as guides, guardians, and sources of inspiration for those who seek their wisdom. Some ascended spirits even become agents of transformation, assisting earthbound loved ones on their path to liberation.

This interplay between the physical world and the

spiritual realm is a constant dance of energies. The actions, intentions, and thoughts of the living have the power to influence and shape the experiences of our departed loved ones. Through our love, compassion, and understanding, we can contribute to the freeing of our earthbound loved ones and foster a deeper connection with our departed ascended spirits.

CHAPTER 4

Embracing the Eternal Connection

AS WE JOURNEY THROUGH life, one inevitable truth we must confront is the loss of our loved ones. The pain and grief that accompany their departure can feel overwhelming, leaving us yearning for a way to maintain a connection with them even after they have transitioned into the realm of the afterlife. During these challenging times, messages from beyond can provide a sense of comfort and healing, as well as offer reassurance or guidance. Together, we will explore various experiences that offer the possibility of connecting with those we hold dear.

Regardless of your beliefs in mediumship, what remains constant across the living is the importance of honoring the memories we have with our departed loved ones. Creating rituals, such as lighting candles, placing photographs, or writing letters, can provide a tangible way to maintain a connection with those who have departed. Engaging in activities that were meaningful for both parties during their lifetime can also evoke a sense of continued presence and shared experiences.

Dreams are another realm where communication between the living and the deceased can occur. In the dream state, our consciousness is free from the constraints of the physical world, allowing us to connect with the spiritual realm more easily. Many report vivid dreams in which they have engaged in conversations or shared moments with their departed loved ones. These dreams often feel incredibly real and can provide comfort, healing, and a sense of continued connection, love, protection, and even warnings.

As we venture into mediumship connections for those left behind, we discover that memories are the golden threads that bind us to the departed and the most common communications shared across the veil. They serve as bridges between the past and the present, allowing us to relive cherished moments spent with our loved ones.

Departed souls also keep their spirits alive and present by sending signs and synchronicities. I am always thrilled to learn of all the different messages loved ones have received from beyond the veil. These signs can take various forms, such as moving objects that hold personal significance, playing a song that contains a special message or reminds them of their loved one, sending a particular animal associated with the departed family member or friend, creating odd electrical occurrences, as well as producing unexplained sounds and feelings. While skeptics may dismiss these occurrences as mere coincidences, those who embrace the possibility of a connection with the afterlife understand that these are how our loved ones communicate with us.

Sometimes, even our ascended departed loved ones send messages to resolve unresolved issues or unfinished business from their time on Earth. These messages serve as an opportunity for reconciliation, forgiveness, or closure. They may help us understand and come to terms with aspects of their life that were left unresolved before their passing. By receiving and acknowledging these messages, we can find healing and closure for ourselves and our departed loved ones.

During difficult times or pivotal moments in our lives, our beloved find they can manifest messages as intuitive insights, giving us a sense of inner knowing. By paying attention to these messages, we can tap into their wisdom and make choices aligned with their guidance.

It is crucial to understand that each person's experience of the afterlife and their ability to connect with the departed is unique. Establishing and nurturing this connection requires patience, trust, and a willingness to embrace the unknown.

Whether through cherished memories, personal rituals, spiritual practices, signs, synchronicities, or professional guidance, remember that love serves as the eternal thread that binds us together. It is powerful and enduring, and death does not sever this connection. It transforms it into a different form of existence and creates the bridge that reaches into the eternal realm, forever uniting us.

CHAPTER 5

Transcending Tragedy: A Journey Beyond Untimely, Tragic, and Violent Deaths

THE TRANSITION FROM LIFE to death is a mysterious passage that every living being must eventually face. However, when death arrives suddenly and violently, it sends shockwaves through the very fabric of our existence. It shatters the fragile balance between life and the great unknown, leaving behind a trail of additional unanswered questions and grieving hearts for those who depart from this world prematurely through untimely, tragic, or violent circumstances: What becomes of their spirits after such devastating experiences? Do they find solace? Do they transcend the pain and darkness that surrounded their earthly departure? As we delve into the realms beyond, we discover a glimmer of hope within these tragic endings.

When a life is abruptly cut short, the immediate aftermath can be disorienting. The spirit, untethered from its physical form, may initially linger near the scene of its demise, bound by the weight of its tragic end. Feelings of confusion, disbelief, and unfinished business can envelop the departed soul, preventing it from moving forward on its spiritual journey.

The spirits of those who suffered a violent or traumatic end often carry residual emotional imprints. Their journey beyond the veil involves a delicate process of release and forgiveness. As they confront the intense emotions that linger, they are gently encouraged to let go of anger, resentment, and despair.

The universe has a way of healing even the deepest wounds. Spiritual guides, angels, and compassionate beings assigned to aid souls in transition appear to offer comfort and guidance. These ethereal guides emanate compassion and understanding, gently coaxing the anguished spirit away from the pain that has consumed them. With delicate nudges, they encourage the spirit to release this pain, helping them to embrace the next phase of their existence.

As the spirit relinquishes this attachment and moves forward, it is important to understand that the energy generated by untimely, tragic, or violent deaths does not define the soul's eternal essence. While the manner of death may seemingly leave scars upon the spirit, the divine nature within each being is resilient and capable of transcendence.

The process of healing is not instantaneous, nor is it linear. Each spirit moves at its own pace, unraveling the layers of pain and anger that have encased it. In this ethereal realm, time loses its relevance as the spirit seeks to uncover the lessons hidden within its tragic fate. With each step forward, the spirit becomes lighter, and its energy shines ever brighter. The universe, in its infinite wisdom, provides a continuous comforting presence, helping the spirit process the events by providing the spirit with opportunities for introspection, reflection, and growth.

These spirits are not restricted by the circumstances of their death but rather enriched by the lessons learned through their experiences. This realm enables them to confront the traumas that marked their untimely death and nurture their emotional wounds toward forgiveness and inner peace. Ultimately, these spirits find liberation and a sense of purpose as they continue their eternal journey beyond the veil.

Along this transformative journey, the spirits may encounter others who suffered similar fates. Together, they form an unbreakable bond, a support network of kindred souls who share their experiences and provide strength throughout this healing process. They become beacons of hope for one another, proving that even the most devastating circumstances can be transcended.

As these spirits reach their highest being, they come to understand their death was not a punishment or a reflection of worth but rather a catalyst for growth and a lesson for the collective consciousness. They use their newfound wisdom to support loved ones left behind.

As the following stories highlight, spirits often seek connections when their earthly journey ends with matters left unresolved. Whether it's an unspoken apology, an undelivered message to set the record straight, or a sense of responsibility left unfulfilled, as you will see from these connections, these spirits seek an avenue to convey their lingering sentiments.

My Daughter's Six-Lane Highway

Melissa came to me to connect to her unique and beautiful daughter, who passed away at the age of 20. Little did I know at the time of her session how special this connection would become.

As soon as I called to her daughter, she came forward with very strong emotions and said, "I want to set the record straight."

Melissa and her mother, who joined her for the session, began asking questions to clarify what happened to her daughter. It was clear to me from the start that her daughter's answers told a very different story than what the authorities, who ruled her daughter's death as a suicide, shared with them.

At that point, her daughter stopped answering their questions and began to show me a step-by-step account of what occurred. She wanted it to be very clear that this was NOT at her own hands like it stated on her death certificate.

She began her account by telling me that she was fighting with her boyfriend while they were driving down a six-lane highway. She stated they were both screaming at each other, and he was hitting her in the head. She told him it was over, and she wanted to get out of the car because she felt like he was going to kill her.

She released her seat belt and held onto the door handle as he slowed down and pushed her out of the car. As she was falling, he accelerated, and as the door was closing, it hit her on the right side of her head. She then hit the back of her head when she fell to the ground.

Very disoriented, she stood up, facing the six-lane highway divided by a median. Unfortunately, her daughter then showed me the steep cliff embankment where she stood, and the only way for her to get off the highway was to attempt to cross all six lanes to reach the other side.

Melissa's daughter let me know that because this happened during the early morning hours, she believed she could cross the lanes safely as there was not a lot of traffic. At that point, her mother confirmed that she was left on a six-lane highway by her boyfriend and that it occurred around 2:00 am.

As her daughter continued, she showed me how she tried to walk across the highway and fell, only to get up and try again, only to fall again. As she attempted to regain her balance, one car hit her, sending her into the air onto an oncoming vehicle. Her daughter confirmed it was the second impact that led to her immediate death.

Her mother quickly confirmed her daughter was hit by two cars but shared with me that the boyfriend's and the eyewitnesses' statements were very different. Her mother then recounted what she was told happened to her daughter in the early morning hours of February 19th.

Melissa let me know her daughter was reported missing by her boyfriend, and during his interview, he said they were at a house where someone was giving her daughter a hard time, so he left to take her home. However, while driving, he claimed an argument erupted between them, and she wanted to get out of the car. He then pulled over and let her out on a six-lane highway. As she walked in the opposite direction, he said he got back into the car and drove away. When he arrived home, he went right to sleep without letting anyone know where she was.

Her mother then continued and shared that the eyewitness testimony claimed they saw her daughter in the middle of the road, and despite their attempts to get her to get into their cars, one said she laid down on the road, and other stated she knelt in a praying motion before being hit by two vehicles.

However, her daughter quickly told me she was not praying or lying down on the road; she was confused, dizzy, and trying to get across the highway. At that point, her daughter's sadness and angry energy began to melt, knowing she was finally able to tell her mom the truth. Melissa quickly confirmed that her family always knew in their hearts this was not a suicide because her daughter had big, big plans, and she was looking forward to her future. Not to mention how many people her daughter had helped stay alive who wanted to end their lives. Melissa said, "I always knew they had it all wrong, but now I know for sure."

Her daughter then showed me a large group of individuals who came to say goodbye to her, and her mother confirmed this by sharing with me that over 1,000 people attended her funeral, and the funeral director said, in his entire career, he had never seen so many come to pay their respects.

As the session continued, her daughter brought forward her concerns about her brother's anger. Melissa confirmed her daughter's concern by letting me know that her brother was having a difficult time with the accident and worried about his sister being with "dark spirits" because of the claim she committed suicide.

Melissa then asked her daughter for a specific sign that would make sense to him so he could know she was ok. Her daughter immediately brought forward an image of a shoe with a hole in the toe and said this was her brother's shoe. Melissa acknowledged that she had bought him shoes not too long ago because of the hole in the toe and even sent a picture of it after the session.

Her daughter then spoke about the Bible verse Matthew 17:20 and wanted her mother to share this message with her brother, again to let him know she was okay. It wasn't until Melissa confirmed the significance of this message that I understood how important it was. Melissa shared with me that her son reads the Bible every night, and it was obvious what her beautiful daughter wanted her brother to know. In layman's terms, the verse means that if you have faith at all, then you should believe in me and that I'm okay.

Then her daughter showed me the inside of her right forearm and gestured towards her mother. I then asked Melissa what she had on the inside of her inner right forearm. She smiled and said they both had gotten matching tattoos the Saturday before Mother's Day a year earlier. The tattoos were written in Greek slang and read, "You are my Sunshine."

At this point in the session, her daughter's goal was to make sure her mother and grandmother knew it was her providing this information, and she didn't want anyone to question that. She spoke about her linked paperclips that her mother now had, rainbows on the floor, and that she leaves shiny pennies for her mother to find.

It didn't take long for Melissa to confirm she had her daughter's jar of linked paperclips, the rainbows that appeared out of nowhere on the floor, and the one shiny penny in her car.

As the session started to wind down, Melissa's daughter showed me an image of the characters from the cartoon Shimmer & Shine. Her daughter focused on their hair color, which was pink and blue. Her mother thought this was amazing because her daughter had bright pink hair, and her mother's hair had purple on the ends at the time of the session.

However, it was the picture of the characters standing together that touched her heart because it looked just like the tattoo that her daughter designed, which she got a year after her daughter's death on the same date they got their Mother's Day tattoos one year earlier.

At the very end of the session, Melissa's daughter kept repeating the phrase, "Stop with the last 2 minutes."

When I first mentioned these words, Melissa didn't know what her daughter meant. But her daughter kept repeating it over and over again and then added, "Stop thinking about those 2 minutes over and over."

Her mother finally understood her daughter's message. Melissa explained that ever since she heard her daughter's account of what happened earlier in the session, she had been replaying the last 2 minutes of her life repeatedly in her head.

She said, "I feel guilty because I couldn't save my daughter, and that's why I keep replaying those last two minutes."

I immediately shared her daughter's reply, "You weren't supposed to."

Before we ended the session, Melissa let me know that nothing will ever bring her daughter back and her heart has been shattered in a million pieces knowing she will never be in this physical world to hug her, kiss her, talk to her, hear her voice, interact with her, and have the privilege of watching her grow older. However, this connection brought her a level of comfort she didn't know existed in her new reality, and validation that even though she is not in the physical world any longer, she now knows her daughter is always with her.

Fatal McDonald's Run

The moment I connected to this spirit, I knew it would be a difficult and emotional session. A male teenager came forward saying how sorry he was that he didn't listen to his girlfriend, whom he loved very much, who had asked him not to go on a McDonald's run because he had been drinking at a party. He then let me know he passed away just a short time later from a fatal two-car motor vehicle accident where he lost control of his car, crashing into another car. He showed me how he had to be cut out of his vehicle because he was pinned inside by the steering wheel. When I asked him to provide something specific to help his loved ones identify him, I began to smell smoke, and he shared that the month of June was significant, as well as the numbers 19 and 23.

Almost immediately, Taryn said this was her 16-year-old high school classmate who passed away in a fatal two-car accident that occurred after he left a party intoxicated to get McDonald's. She then confirmed that his girlfriend begged him not to go, and he luckily left her behind at the party. Taryn then shared that her friend was cut out of the vehicle because the front end of his car was crushed, which caused the car to catch on fire, melting the seatbelt to his body and pinning him behind the steering wheel. She also confirmed that June was his parents' anniversary month, that 19 was his football number, and that 23 was his basketball number.

Black Ice, Not Speed

A young woman who was in her early 20s came forward. She passed in a motor vehicle accident as she was going home during the colder months of the year. It was very clear to me that she wanted to set the record straight and let her loved ones know how the accident occurred. She stated that her car hit black ice, and the icy roadway caused her car to run off the road and hit a wooden pole, not speed. She then showed me her head injury and talked about the internal bleeding that ended her life. She then shared with me that April was a significant month to her, as well as the numbers 23 and 17.

However, when I asked her to give me one specific detail that would help her family know it was her, the young woman showed me a blue tattoo on the inside of her right forearm.

Anastasia immediately let me know this was her niece, who passed away in a car accident at the age of 23 by running off the road and hitting a big wooden fence pole as she was on her way home. Anastasia then confirmed the tattoo on the inside of her right forearm was of a blue jay, and April 17th was her son's birthday. But when Anastasia started to talk about how the accident occurred, it was clear to me how important it was for her to receive confirmation about the icy roadway.

It turned out that the authorities said her niece was speeding. This accusation led to others saying very hateful things about her niece and caused a lot of turmoil for the family. However, the family didn't believe she was driving too fast, and Anastasia was grateful to learn her family was right all along.

A 12-Year-Old's Final Act

This was one of the most heartbreaking spirit connections I have experienced, not only because of the spirit's age but also because she took her life. When I started this connection, it was clear this was a young child who died by suicide. She spoke about suffering from depression, bullying, and personal challenges that resulted in her difficult passing. At this point, she focused on a facial deformity of her mouth that caused her to speak funny and led to bullying and making her feel like an alien. She then spoke about the numbers 9 and 11, a bird with a yellow belly, patchwork clothing, the singer Taylor Swift, milk in her hair, and the words "I'm sorry" to her mom and brother echoed in my head.

Not a minute went by when Samantha said she was shaking because she knew this was her best friend's daughter, who was just 12 years old and passed away on November 9. It turned out they had only said their final goodbyes two days earlier. Samantha confirmed this child did have a severe overbite, which affected her speech, leading to bullying and depression.

Unfortunately, this beautiful little girl ended her life in her home, where her mother and brother found her.

Because of the sensitivity of this connection and many of the details Samantha could not confirm, I asked if I could connect directly to her mom, Amber.

I was delighted when her mother, Amber, agreed to continue the connection to her daughter as part of her healing process. Just days later, during the connection with her mother, she was able to confirm many of the details her daughter shared, but her friend Samantha could not confirm.

During the connection with her mom, her daughter, calling her mama, told her, "I finally got to see Taylor Swift front and center."

With sweet sadness in her voice and wiping away tears, her mom said she was glad because her daughter loved Taylor Swift.

Amber then picked up a blue rubber chicken with a yellow stress ball for a head and a yellow guitar on its belly and said, "This is the bird with the yellow belly her daughter made and spoke about in the connection with Samantha."

She then went on to confirm the patchwork clothing was the skirts she wears all the time.

Unfortunately, the connection to her mom also allowed her daughter to share a few additional heart-breaking moments about when and where she would decide to commit this act. Her daughter told me that the last time she remembered being happy was at the age of 9, and this was why she chose the 9th to take her life, as she wanted to be remembered for when she was last happy. Then, she shared how she thought about where she was going to end her life. She explained to me how she was going to leave the house to do this so they wouldn't find her, but then she didn't want her mom to worry and think she was missing and decided it was best to stay in the home and do it there.

Amber confirmed that when her daughter was nine years old, her sister was still in the home, and she was happy. She then continued to explain that was the connection to the milk in her hair. It was her sister who poured milk in her hair in the kitchen after she poured water on her sister's hair.

Amber also confirmed that in her daughter's journal, she wrote about going into the woods to commit her final act but decided not to.

It was a bittersweet moment for me as we ended the connection now having answered why, where, and when her little girl chose to take her life. It is my hope that her mom finds comfort in knowing her daughter is no longer being bullied and is happy again.

Always a Nurse

This young 20-something-year-old spirit came forward, speaking about losing control of her car on black ice and running off the road hitting a tree. She said it was a fatal accident, and she passed from a severe head injury. When she appeared to me, she was wearing a white nurse's uniform and highlighted the end of December and beginning of January, along with the number 28.

It only took a moment for Emily to let me know this was her sister, who passed away the week of New Year's by running off the road and hitting a tree on her way to a nursing placement in her uniform. Emily then confirmed that there was a light frost, making the roads very slippery at the time of her accident. Her sister passed away when Emily was just 28 and left behind her mom, dad, and sister. Emily was grateful to learn the truth about what happened to her sister.

Speed was a Factor

During this spirit connection, a male spirit came forward and described a motorcycle accident where speed was his only error and claimed the accident was not his fault. Through images, he showed me how he was thrown off his bike, suffering a severe head injury and a bent thumb. As the session continued, he provided the dates of October 1st and 11th, as well as shared how important the month of May was to him. The last words he said, "Tell the love of my life that our hearts will always beat together."

It didn't take long for his fiancé to claim this was her best friend and the love of her life that she met in May, and they were engaged on October 11th. She went on to confirm that he passed from a brain injury and suffered a broken thumb as a result of being thrown from his motorcycle in an accident that occurred on October 1st.

His fiancé explained why he claimed the accident was not his fault. It turns out he did speed up to go around and pass a driver on the left, however, the accident was seemingly caused by the other driver, who, without looking, proceeded to make a U-turn and before he could respond, T-boned him and the motorcycle.

His fiancé then shared she was with him the entire time at the hospital and listened to his heart's last beat as she let him go. She was overjoyed knowing he knew she was there by his last statement and said, "My heart is so full right now!"

your loved ones are always with you

Left for Dead

———

A young adult male came forward and immediately stated that this was a random crime committed against him and not his doing. He then showed me that he was left outside between two buildings near a roadway. I could even hear the cars driving by at the same time he revealed that he suffered a head injury and abdominal internal bleeding, which took his life.

As the connection continued, he spoke about the significance of the months of May and August, as well as the number 11.

Because this was a crime, I wanted to ensure a quick connection and asked for him to show me something that would instantly let his loved one know it was him. A moment later, he showed me a picture of Snoopy from The Peanuts cartoon.

It didn't take long for his niece to let me know this was her uncle who was killed and left for dead in between two buildings near a roadway. She went on to confirm he suffered from a head injury, as well as internal bleeding—just as he stated.

It turns out that May was her mother's (his sister's)

birthday and August 11 was his birthday. But it was the Snoopy detail that made all the difference for her because the image of Snoopy was on his headstone.

She was so grateful for this connection but wished for him to know that his granddaughters loved him even though they never had a chance to meet him. Knowing how important it was for her to know he was with them before this wonderful spirit said goodbye, he let her know that he sends all of them rainbows through a particular crystal light. Immediately, she confirmed this crystal light in her home with its sparkling rainbows and cried.

your loved ones are always with you

All Together

A young adult male and a little boy he called "little guy" came forward together. The adult male spoke about the two of them being in a car accident, where they were hit by a drunk driver who ran a red light. He let me know that his car was hit on the driver's side at full speed, requiring him to be cut from the vehicle with the jaws of life. He also spoke about the head injury he suffered when his head hit the window and showed me a child seat in the back of the car. He then brought forward the month of July and the number 3, along with the beautiful message of love, and said, "Please tell her we are all happy and together, watching over everyone."

Johnson immediately let me know this was her brother and 3-year-old nephew who passed away when a drunk driver ran through a red light. She confirmed they were cut from the vehicle and suffered fatal injuries. She then went on to confirm that her dad called her nephew "little guy," and that her birthday was in July, and this was the last time she saw them. She was so happy to learn that they were together and happy watching over the family.

Wrong Place Wrong Time

A young adult male came forward, letting me know he was shot more than one time and wanted to make sure his loved ones knew, "This was not my doing. This was done to me. I was just in the wrong place at the wrong time."

He then showed me a two-hole belt and a high stack of advanced schoolbooks. Next, he told me that the month of February was significant, along with the numbers 23 and 28.

Not a moment went by before Noelle let me know this was her cousin, who passed away after being shot at age 23. She confirmed what the family already knew: this was not his doing, and how he was mistakenly shot by men in uniform. She then let me know that his sister had his belt, and the schoolbooks represented her being in college.

However, it was February 28th, his birthday, that let Noelle know he was talking to her, and she could not have been happier to receive his confirming message.

CHAPTER 6

Messages of Love Know No Boundaries

LOVE, BEING A POWERFUL force that transcends the boundaries of life and death, compels spirits to reach out to their beloved. The desire to assure their loved ones of an enduring connection or to provide comfort during times of grief becomes a driving force for these types of ethereal communications.

In the divine tapestry that binds the realms of the living and the departed, the concept that love knows no boundaries takes center stage. Spirits, propelled by the undying force of love, often come forward to communicate with their loved ones to express messages of affection and support.

Spirits, aware of the enduring nature of their feelings, seek to reassure their loved ones that this bond persists beyond the physical realm. Their messages carry echoes of love to provide comfort and offer a gentle reminder that the love shared in life continues to flourish in the spiritual realm. This reassurance becomes a source of healing for those navigating the complex landscape of loss.

Our departed loved ones communicate through emotions, sensations, and shared memories that resonate with those left behind. These subtle expressions serve to heal the wounds in the living and the departed.

In the whispers of our beloved and the subtle signs they impart, we can hear their profound affirmation of love. As we delve into the following spirit communications guided by the principle that love knows no boundaries, we discover these stories unravel this timeless essence of the human connection.

Funny Grandma Lost Her Brain

This session began with a funny grandma coming forward and calling herself "mom." She immediately spoke about the months of May and August, as well as the numbers 15 and 22 as being significant to her. Then she let me know she had cancer and "lost her brain."

When I inquired what she meant by this, she said, "I just wasn't myself in the end."

Grandma then began to make funny sipping noises and brought forward the distinct smell of something burning. As the burning scent disappeared from my awareness, it was quickly replaced by the smell of American fast food.

It didn't take long for Alexandria to recognize this was her very funny grandma, whom she referred to as mom because her grandma raised her. Alexandria confirmed that her grandma did have leukemia, and as she slipped into a coma towards the end of her life she rambled with great confusion.

Alexandria continued to explain the significance of the months and numbers her grandma brought forward. She began by letting me know that May was her birthday month, and the 15th was the day of her grandma's birthday. However, when Alexandra expressed that the 22nd was the day her dad passed and August was the month of grandma's passing, it couldn't be clearer—Grandma was letting Alexandria know they were happily together, watching over her.

Then the session took a funny turn, and I couldn't help but chuckle a bit as Alexandria confirmed the burning smell was grandma burning dinner while the sipping noise was grandma sipping her wine as she always did. But it was that smell of fast food that was most meaningful to Alexandria since she brought her grandma Burger King for the last time not too long before her passing.

As Alexandria recounted each event during the session, all she could say was how much she missed her funny grandma, and all grandma could say was how much she loved and missed her beautiful granddaughter.

your loved ones are always with you

Secret Sauce Grandfather

This grandfather came forward with a special delicious secret that he took to the grave. He began by making fun of the ironic nature of his sudden death. He explained that he passed in his sleep from a heart attack that occurred while he was waiting to have surgery for clogged arteries. He couldn't help but laugh as he described his passing.

He went on to talk about the significance of February and November, along with the numbers 37 and 15. However, it was the mentioning of his special secret barbecue sauce that sealed the deal for Jenna.

Within moments, Jenna knew without a doubt that this was her grandfather, and confirmed he passed in his sleep from a heart attack while awaiting heart surgery. She then went on to confirm he passed on February 15, his birthday was in November, and that her mom's age was 37 at the time of his passing. But when she began to speak about his famous barbecue sauce, her joy warmed my heart. Jenna let me know that he was famous for this recipe and made it for every occasion, but unfortunately never wrote it down.

Throughout the session, Jenna could not hold back her love for her grandfather, and her grandfather expressed his love right back by showing me hearts that surrounded his every word. However, she wished he would have come back to give her that recipe and hopes maybe one day he will.

your loved ones are always with you

Happy Birthday Grandson

This sweet spirit that called herself mom came forward to connect with her daughter and deliver a very special message. She began by revealing she passed from cancer that started in her female organs and spread as she battled this disease over time. Then she quickly showed me a chocolate cake with a birthday candle and let me know that the months of October and May were significant, along with the number 13.

It didn't take long for Cari to let me know this was her mom. She confirmed that May was her brother's birthday and her mom passed on the 13th. Then she confirmed her mom passed from cancer that spread quickly within her body. However, it was the chocolate cake with a birthday candle that brought tears to her eyes. Cari revealed that she had just ordered a chocolate cake today for her son's October birthday, which was the following day. At that moment she happily realized her sweet mom came to wish her son a Happy Birthday.

2 Slices of Pecan Pie, Please

A joyful grandpa immediately spoke about issues with his feet being swollen, sores, and not healing—along with out-of-control diabetes despite trying many medications to get it under control. He said, "It just kept getting worse no matter what I did."

He cheerfully let me know that his family was with him when he passed and how much he loved his wife and her homemade pecan pie. He then let me know the month of August was significant, as well as the numbers 8 and 21.

Ann-Marie identified this happy spirit as her grandpa and quickly confirmed that he had diabetes that could not be controlled with medication, which led to sores on his swollen feet. However, she said, "That didn't stop him from eating two or three slices of my grandma's pecan pie she always made for him, because it was his favorite."

Unfortunately, Ann-Marie let me know that his diabetes did result in him losing his ability to walk and he passed on August 8th surrounded by her grandma, whose birthday is on July 21st, and her two aunts. She was grateful to learn he was still watching over her.

Pepsi with a Side of Red Meat

During this spirit connection, a colorful grandpa came forward in all his glory. He spoke about how he loved to smoke, eat, and drink. His favorite meal would include a Pepsi and some type of red meat.

He said, "I'm sure it was to no one's surprise that I went out with a heart attack."

Then he brought to my attention how much he loved his daughter and was sorry he missed out on most of her life. He finished the connection by letting me know the month of July as well as the numbers 13 and 21 were significant to him.

This comedic spirit was quickly identified by Jodie as her dad. She confirmed that everyone told him to stop his way of life, but he didn't. She jokingly said, "They told us he was gone before he hit the floor."

Jodie then went on to explain July 21st was the day he passed, and she was just 13 years old at the time. She was taken aback to learn even after all these years he was still present in her life, watching over her, and that he never lost his sense of humor.

Wrangler Shirt Pillow of Love

A dad came forward calling himself a weekend fisherman and proudly showed me his tackle box, long boots, and him standing in the river. He then explained how he didn't like or go to doctors, but he became very sick from an infection and had no choice but to go see a doctor.

Unfortunately, he let me know he went to the doctor too late and passed away from becoming septic from the infection. He then showed me a light blue shirt with buttons and seemed to hug it, leaving me a bit confused.

He then talked about the month of November, along with the numbers 11 and 12.

Aly immediately said this was her weekend fisherman dad, whose birthday was November 11th. She confirmed his dislike for doctors and that he did pass from a septic infection on April 12th. However, when I asked her about the light blue shirt with buttons, she said proudly and with love, "It's his wrangler shirt I got made into a pillow. I'm so glad he knows I did that for him."

your loved ones are always with you

Two Peas in a Pod

This young adult female spirit came forward with the most beautiful loving energy. She desperately wanted to connect to her best friend describing the two of them as two peas in a pod. She began by providing details of having cancer as a child and then having it come back to take her life as an adult. It was clear to me as she spoke, she and her friend had shared a lot throughout her life journey.

As the spirit continued to try and connect to her best friend, she spoke about the months of May, June, and July, as well as the numbers 20 and 27. Then she said, "Tell her I love her."

A moment later, a woman with the username Southern Style acknowledged this was her best friend who passed at age 27 from revenge brain cancer after having beat leukemia as a child.

Southern Style then confirmed what only she and her best friend could know—the significance of the months and numbers her friend shared. June was the month her best friend found out she was pregnant, July was the month her daughter was expected to be born, and May 20th was the day her daughter was born. This made it clear to Southern Style that her best friend wanted her to connect to her daughter to let her know her mom was with her, watching over her, and has always loved her very much.

Trickster Best Friend

During this spirit connection, a female calling herself a friend came forward, making me feel like I couldn't take a breath and was drowning from the inside. She then gave me the painful feeling of having an IV needle stuck into my left wrist so I couldn't move it without pain, all while telling me she passed alone and referencing the month of May. However, when she spoke about "picking bones out of a fish with love", I knew this was going to be a beautiful connection.

Jennifer quickly confirmed this was her good friend who had passed in May alone in the hospital from Covid with an IV in her left wrist. Jennifer also confirmed that they would eat lunch together at work and she would often eat fish with bones she needed to pick out.

The sweetest part of the connection came when Jennifer asked if her friend knew about her fiancé. Her friend quickly spoke about how happy she was for Jennifer and how much she watches her fiancé watch her with love. Jennifer's friend even talked about how her fiance thinks it's cute that she walks on her toes, and Jennifer of course confirmed this was true.

Then her friend spoke about her fiancé's toothbrush, the one that she had purposely dropped into the sink, then onto the floor because it was too hard for her finance's bleeding gums. Then she stated her fiancé needed to go to the dentist. Jennifer could not hold back and said, "OMG! Yes, he has bleeding gums. I begged my fiancé to go to the dentist for some time with no luck."

However, when Jennifer asked if it was her friend who had been making her fiancé's shirt dance. Her friend quickly answered, "Yes, and I also move things around your home only to put them back in the same place after you search everywhere for them."

Her friend also admitted she was the one who was knocking things down to the ground and playing odd music.

Jennifer confirmed each of these things were occurring in her home and let me know, "It all made perfect sense because she had always been a trickster, and now I know nothing has changed."

Cheese Doodle Hands

The young woman came forward and told her story of having passed by suffering a fatal head injury in a multi-car collision. She spoke about the month of February and September as being significant to her, as well as the number 21. But the surprise detail that came forward during this reading was the image of orange hands and her speaking about her love of Cheese Doodles.

The connection was made to her niece who confirmed that her aunt had died at the age of 21 because of a severe head injury she suffered in a two-car accident. She also confirmed that the accident took place in September and her birthday was in February.

However, my favorite part of the reading was when her niece confirmed her love of Cheese Doodles and let me know that when her aunt was little, she thought it was so funny how the Cheese Doodles made her hands turn orange and would laugh as she looked at them. Her niece was glad to learn her aunt was okay and still laughing about the Cheese Doodles.

Orange-Filled Milk Chocolate

———

This connection brought forward a sweet older woman who referred to herself as mom and grandma. The very first thing she showed me was a white box with orange-filled chocolates inside. She then spoke about having chest pain and difficulty breathing. To me, it felt like my chest was filling with fluid and I couldn't take a breath. She then brought to my attention the months of May and February and the numbers 10 and 86. However, when I asked her to show me something very specific, she showed me plates with gold edging and said, "She will know them."

For Angie, it was clear this was her mother-in-law. She immediately confirmed the milk chocolates filled with orange filling that came in a white box was something her mother-in-law ordered from a catalog by the case, since she loved them so much. The plates were something Angie had just moved and was so delighted to know that her mother-in-law was watching over her in this way. She then confirmed that her mother-in-law passed from heart failure and her great-grandchildren's birthdays were May 10 and February 10, and her granddaughter was born in the year 1986.

Mints On the Bill

A female spirit came forward letting me know she passed from breast cancer that had spread through her lymphatic system throughout her body despite the surgeries she endured and being a part of a clinical trial. She talked about this being a long journey, but unfortunately, nothing worked.

Then she let me know she was under hospice care before she passed, and her family was with her during her final moments. At this point, this beautiful spirit brought forward the months of May and June, and the number 27 as significant.

At the end of the connection, she referenced Olive Garden and Andie's chocolates, which made me know there had to be a story waiting to be told.

It didn't take long for Tracy to identify this spirit as her sister-in-law who had a long battle with breast cancer that spread throughout her body even though she tried everything to fight it. She also confirmed her sister-in-law was receiving hospice care and the family was with her at the time of her passing. Tracy then confirmed that her sister-in-law passed on June 27 and the last family birthday celebrations she attended were in May.

However, laughter took over the conversation when Tracy spoke about Olive Garden. As it turned out there was only one Olive Garden in town, and it was the only place they ate together. Tracy shared that whenever the bill came, they would always fight over the Andie's candies that came with the bill. She was happy to learn her sister-in-law was watching over her.

your loved ones are always with you

Mom's 7-Year Battle

This beautiful mom came forward talking about her long battle with cancer and how much pain she was in as she spent her last moments in hospice care telling the loved ones surrounding her that, "It's time to let go."

She expressed how grateful she was for her family's help during her final days and acknowledged how June and November were significant months for her, along with the numbers 7, 12, and 20.

The last detail she shared to help make this connection personal was to show me images of an array of multi-colored candy canes and let me know she comes to her daughter on the right side with a bit of a chill causing her daughter goosebumps.

Within a moment her daughter came forward to claim this spirit as her mom. She quickly confirmed her mom had a 7-year-long battle with cancer and she ended her life surrounded by loved ones under hospice care.

Her daughter then went on to confirm June was her mom's birthday month and November 20th was her older sister's birthday. She then let me know that her mom had said she wanted to go home, and all 12 of her children and her dad told her, "Yes, it's okay to go home," as they didn't want her to suffer anymore.

Her daughter then shared that her mom's favorite candy was multi-colored candy canes and she passed away watching a movie surrounded by all her loved ones.

Before I ended the session, the daughter let me know, "I absolutely feel chills on my right side and that is where I have her name tattoo, now I know she is always with me."

Rosary in My Hands

This kind warm spirit came to me saying she was a mom who passed away from a combination of lung disease and breathing complications from a lung infection that caused fluid to build up in her lungs. She then let me know before she went through a very difficult passing, she was on oxygen in the ICU with family. Then, this mom spoke about her daughter holding her left hand with her two hands cradling a rosary, leaning forward, crying after she passed.

After that moment, she let me feel a small gold cross she placed on my chest and showed me that May and June were significant months to her.

Not a moment went by before Diana claimed this spirit as her mom. She quickly confirmed that her mom passed from a long-term lung disease that was complicated by fluid in the lungs. Diana then confirmed she was with her mom as she went through a difficult passing in the ICU, as she cupped her mom's left hand in hers while holding a rosary.

Diana then went on to say, "Yes, I did place the rosary cross on her chest, leaned forward, and cried over her hand as I held it."

Diana continued to let me know that the month of May was her daughter's birthday and June was when her mom's dad and brother passed.

I explained to Diana this was her mom's way of letting her know they were happily all together and watching over her.

your loved ones are always with you

The Kugel Grandmother

During this connection a female came forward who called herself Grandma. This spirit started the connection by talking about her swollen feet which made it difficult for her to walk and the fall she took in her home, where she hit the front right side of her head causing her brain to bleed.

She then spoke about the months of May and June, along with the numbers 86 and 21. But it was the noodle dish which she called Kugel that convinced Rachel this was her grandmother.

Immediately Rachel confirmed that May was her birthday month, June was her mother's and her son's birthday, and that her grandmother passed at age 86 when Rachel was just 21 years old. But the confirmation didn't stop there, Rachel went on to let me know that her grandmother did have swollen feet that made it difficult for her to walk and that she had fallen in her living room where she was found on the floor, after hitting the front side of her head.

The sweetest moment during this connection came when Rachel confirmed that her grandmother loved to make all kinds of food and Kugel was one of her favorites.

CHAPTER 7

Messages of Healing and Closure

THE EXCHANGE OF HEALING messages between the beloved and the living aids the departed in their spiritual voyage while providing a well of strength for those left behind. These messages offer ongoing support that guides the living through challenges and decisions they must now face alone.

These messages from our beloved hold the capacity to nurture a union that overcomes the physical separation, bringing healing and closure to those who receive them. At the very core of these communications lies the emotional, psychological, and spiritual well-being that contributes significantly to this healing process.

When a loved one passes away, it leaves an emptiness that often ignites grief and longing, accompanied by feelings of loss and disconnection. It is these messages that serve as a bridge to fill the void, offering a sense of reassurance that our loved ones are still with us.

When those who are left behind receive messages

from departed loved ones, it can be a cathartic experience. The very act of receiving these messages creates healing through validation of the enduring bond they share. This continued connection can soothe feelings of isolation, easing the burden of grief.

Healing, through these ongoing connections, brings forward the emotional comfort that comes with the acknowledgment that their relationship continues. These messages often convey love, forgiveness, and understanding, while addressing unresolved emotions that accompany the grieving process. Knowing that the relationship they cherished remains intact on a spiritual level, for many, allows deep-seated emotions to be released.

Closure, on the other hand, brings about clarity and acceptance of what occurred. It is not merely about tying up loose ends. These messages promote insights that lead to inner peace, and dispelling doubts. Many times, these connections result in the living receiving apologies, expressions of love, and even guidance. All of which provide those left behind a sense of resolution for lingering questions and uncertainties they may be holding onto. This closure becomes their foundation to rebuild their lives and navigate the complexities of grief, finding resolution and peace in the face of loss.

The power of these messages extends beyond healing and closure. They inspire personal growth and often carry a transformative energy that instills a sense of purpose. This purpose often leads to positive acts of honor in the memory of their beloved. It motivates them to channel their grief into positive actions, restoring balance to their lives.

Ultimately, grieving is a deeply personal and often complex process. Spirits seek communication to offer a sense of peace to those left behind. Through these messages, spirits can be instrumental in facilitating healing and closure, both for themselves and their loved ones. The reassurance that they are still connected, allows for this mutual process that transcends the boundaries between realms.

The following stories of connection focus on shared beautiful moments of healing and closure taking place between those left behind and loved ones who have crossed over.

Hidden Truth

As grandma came forward, I began to have trouble breathing, experienced pain in my head, and the feeling that something was wrong with my throat. She then spoke about a red seat, her daughter remembering her granddaughter's hands, and her wish that came true when her granddaughter did not witness her difficult passing. However, when the grandma spoke about a family member drawing her headstone, I couldn't wait to understand why.

Her granddaughter immediately confirmed that her grandma suffered a stroke only one week before she arrived in Portugal and that she had a difficult passing filled with haunting noises as she struggled to breathe. Her granddaughter felt blessed that her grandma had protected her from being there and watching her pass in such a manner.

However, it was her grandma's reference to the red seat that brought her granddaughter so much understanding and healing. Prior to her granddaughter's trip to Portugal, her mother suffered an aneurysm, which resulted in severe memory loss. Before this connection, she couldn't understand why her grandma did not try to remind her mother about her existence and was sad her grandma wasn't alive when they reconnected.

But, once the grandma spoke of the red seat, the granddaughter realized her grandma was with her in spirit at the restaurant where she sat in the red seat across from her mom, seeing her for the first time since her aneurysm.

The granddaughter confirmed what her grandma shared was true. Her mom did recognize her through her hands because they looked just like her mom's, and this triggered the beginning memories of her for her mom.

But this wonderful connection was deepened even further when her granddaughter explained her aunt drew her grandma's headstone to show her what it was going to look like because she had to return home to the US and was not going to be there to see it. This was the moment she knew, without a doubt, that not only was her grandma watching out for her when she was alive, but that she was also watching over her now.

Blanket of Flowers

———

The session began with a woman coming forward calling herself sister. She immediately let me know she suffered from mental issues and depression, which led to her taking her own life. She showed me a chain with a small religious gold charm and a blanket that looked like flowers sewn together. Then she spoke about the month of May being significant and the month of April being significant for two reasons, as well as the number 18.

A moment later, Patsy confirmed this was her sister who suffered from depression and mental illness and committed suicide. She then confirmed the small gold religious symbol was her small gold cross, the blanket of flowers was a quilt made for her by her granny, May was the month of their older sister's passing and April 18th was her birthday. However, she also confirmed the second reason why April was so important to her sister: "This was the month her first child passed from SIDS."

Her sister then let Patsy know she was truly happy for the first time and that her beautiful child was with her. Patsy was delighted to learn she was happy and now Patsy could be happy too.

your loved ones are always with you

27 Shots, But Over the First

———

This was a difficult spirit connection because the young adult that came forward was killed through violent means. He immediately let me know he was gunned down. He said he had multiple injuries but passed from the first shot. He went on to talk about the months of May and June, along with the numbers 7, 17, and 27. I also asked if he would share something specific about himself. He showed me a tattoo on his upper right arm that was a black and red symbol, and that he was pulling apart a piece of green apple taffy.

It didn't take long for the connection to be made to Heather, who let me know this was her cousin who had just turned 30. She quickly confirmed he had been shot 27 times and they told the family that he passed by the first or second shot because it hit his heart.

She was so happy to have this confirmed and said, "I'm so glad to know this. It's such a huge relief to know this. We had all hoped he didn't suffer."

Heather then confirmed the month and numbers he shared. She let me know he was shot in June 2017, his son was born in July, and his birthday was in May.

She then gave me a glimpse into who he was by sharing that the black and red-letter tattoo was a Chinese symbol meaning hope and that they shared Laffy Taffy as their favorite candy, with his favorite flavor being green apple.

All Together Now

A young adult male came forward who died by suicide because he was in mental distress with severe anxiety, depression, and was very angry. He described feeling like he was always on fire. He also let me know he was being bullied and just couldn't take it anymore. When he began to talk about his passing, he let me know he was using drugs and shot himself in the head to "make sure he didn't come back."

When I asked him to tell me something specific so his family would know it was him, he told me about his specialty knife collection that he loved. Then he let me know that June and the number 17 were significant to him.

It didn't take long for Stacy to claim this spirit as her son. She quickly confirmed he did use drugs and fatally shot himself in the head. She also confirmed that he suffered from mental illness and was always very angry, even as a child. Stacy went on to confirm that before her son's death, she tried to help him with the bullying from his children's mother's family, but it just pushed him over the edge.

She let me know that he got worse after his brothers' passing, and confirmed June was when his younger brother passed, and the number 17 was the day his older brother passed. She asked if they were happy and all together. I was grateful I was able to reassure her that they were.

Then Stacy spoke about his knife collection, and said, "There were so many odd ones that he loved, and I have them all here with me."

Mom Has Her Shoes

This teenager came forward letting me know she was hit at dusk by an older car with square lights while walking on the side of a road that had a very narrow shoulder. She spoke about being thrown out of her white tennis shoes and that she is the one moving the toy that she played with as a child. She also referenced the numbers 5, 7, and 9.

It didn't take long for Barbie to let me know this spirit was her high school best friend whose birthday was May 7, 1990. Barbie also confirmed her friend was hit at dusk by an older car when walking on a narrow road. She then went on to confirm that her friend was thrown out of her white tennis sneakers and that her mom still has her shoes to this day.

The part of this connection that touched my heart was when I answered her friend's mom's question, "Is my daughter moving the light-up toy she had as a child?"

Barbie let me know the question came about because her friend's mom heard a baby sound and went into the room to see it moving.

I was so happy I could confirm it was her daughter with this quote: "Tell my mom, yes that is me, I'm moving it."

your loved ones are always with you

Just a Country Boy

A young male came forward with a medium dog with long fur and long ears. He went on to describe a motor vehicle accident where his car was totaled and he was trapped inside. He then brought forward an older male and began to talk about how close he was to his dad. He continued to tell me how he grew up in the country and that one of his favorite things to do was go fishing in the lake with his dad. He then spoke about the months of June and October as being significant, as well as the numbers 3 and 23.

Kimberly came forward and said this was her brother with his dog. She confirmed her brother passed away 3 days after his 16th birthday in a car accident where he was trapped inside. She went on to confirm that she and her mom's birthdays were in June. Then she confirmed that October was the month he passed away, and if he had lived, he would now be 23.

Kimberly then focused her attention on the older male with her brother. She let me know this was her dad who passed away from a broken heart just one year and three days after her brother's passing. She shared with me that she knew it was him immediately because they were extremely close, and they loved to fish together on the lake. At that moment she said, "I'm so happy to learn they are together again."

Canceled Wedding

This session brought forward a young woman who passed from a severe brain injury she suffered during a head-on collision where she was hit by an impaired driver going the wrong way. She also spoke about chocolate-covered caramels as a favorite of hers and the months of June and November, along with the numbers 28 and 21.

It didn't take long for Maya to claim this spirit as her 28-year-old best friend from childhood. She quickly confirmed that she passed away from a brain injury caused by a head-on collision where the other driver was impaired and going the wrong way. She then let me know chocolate caramels were their favorite candy, but it was when Maya revealed that her friend was supposed to be married on June 21st and that she passed in November, that I couldn't help feeling the sadness her friend expressed having never made it to her wedding.

However, by the end of the session, they shared a sweet goodbye, and her friend was able to let her know she was okay.

Squishmallows, Squishmallows

A young adult woman came to me full of beautiful young energy. She was just glowing even as she spoke about quickly passing from cervical cancer surrounded by family. She wanted to connect to the person who bought her squishmallows "in a cool green color" and acknowledged the months of February and July, along with the number 22.

To my delight, Cat immediately said this was her 37-year-old best friend who passed away from cervical cancer. She confirmed her friend had beautiful young-at-heart energy and that she had asked her to get her a squishmallow stuffed animal before her passing. Cat let me know she got two of them for her, "I have two on my bed right now that I had bought for her before she died. One is that green color and the other has a sparkly tummy."

Then Cat confirmed her friend passed away in July, the last pictures she had with her were in February, and they became best friends in 2022. Cat could not have been happier to learn her friend knew she bought her the squishmallows just like she asked, and that her best friend is still with her.

Watching Over My Girls

A young man came to me talking about a motorcycle accident that occurred at dusk and he was thrown from the bike. He let me know he was there for some time and even made it to the ER, but his internal bleeding was too great, and he passed away. He spoke about being a dad and his baby girls, along with the month of June and the number 25.

Kisto let me know this was her cousin who passed away at the age of 25 after being thrown off a motorcycle and died at the hospital from internal bleeding. However, it was when he spoke about his baby girls that her mind was blown. His wife only learned about being pregnant a second time after his death and always wondered if he knew about her birth.

It turns out, the baby girl was born in June, and this was his way of making sure his wife and his girls knew he was watching over all of them.

Don't Cry Over Spilled Ashes

―――

A father came forward letting me know how skinny he was because he passed away from cancer. He then smiled as he talked about being surrounded by family at the time of his passing.   However, a moment later I heard laughter as he shared, "My ashes went everywhere."

Then he spoke about the months of March and July.

I knew there had to be a funny story behind this one and couldn't wait to hear it. Aimee quickly let me know this was her father who passed away from cancer with his family present. Then she confirmed the month of March was his birthday.

However, when she spoke of July she stopped and said, "This was the month we buried his ashes, but before we did, I spilled his ashes trying to put some into a necklace. I hope he forgives me."

Immediately her father laughed and said, "Of course," while sending lots of love.

CHAPTER 8

Messages of Guidance and Protection

MESSAGES REACHING ACROSS THE veil between the living and the departed can also carry an essence of guidance and protection for those left behind. One significant aspect of these messages is the wisdom, direction, and sense of safeguarding they convey. Departed loved ones, free from the constraints of physical existence, use their broader perspective and deeper insights to send messages of guidance. These insights offer those left behind a feeling of empowerment at moments of uncertainty, helping them navigate the complexities of their life challenges.

The protective nature of these messages often lies in the expressions of concern and acts as a shield against life struggles. For those left behind, this creates a feeling of being watched over during difficult times. The sense of support embedded in these messages empowers their loved ones to face life obstacles with a newfound sense of purpose and determination.

They encourage the living to trust their instincts, embrace their personal strengths, and confront their life hurdles. This empowerment serves to not only guide but to provide their loved ones with the confidence to face life's uncertainties without them.

The following stories focus on these moments of guidance and protection shared by departed loved ones as they watch over those left behind.

Small Flower Assault

A young female spirit came forward claiming she had been attacked and ascended from multiple injuries including a severe head injury. She spoke about a small flower tattoo on her hand and that she knew her attacker. This young adult female spirit also spoke about the importance of the month of April and the number 10. However, when the spirit began to speak about making her loved one feel sick as she was being followed in a parking lot to get her attention, chills took over my entire being.

Within moments, this beautiful spirit was claimed by Brooke, who stated it was her aunt coming forward. Brooke immediately confirmed that her aunt suffered a severe head injury in an attack by a friend who later confessed to this crime in a letter before he took his life. She then went on to confirm her aunt also had a small flower tattoo on her hand and that the month of April is her birthday, and she was only 10 when this crime took place.

Knowing this was her niece, her aunt let her know she had been watching over her all these years. When I asked if she felt her aunt on her upper back on the right side, the niece happily answered yes and shared, "I'm not surprised because that is exactly where I have her name tattooed on my back."

However, when Brooke confirmed that yes, she felt her aunt with her in the parking lot just days ago when someone was following her and it was the sick feeling that brought her attention to the situation, the connection was undeniable.

Stop the Salt

This was a very sweet connection of a dad coming through to connect to his daughter. He began by letting me know he passed away from cancer that was in multiple organs and that he chose to "stop treatment so he could be with his family before he left."

He spoke about the importance of the months of June, December, and January, as well as the number 11. He then showed me an old baseball card and said his daughter needed to stop eating so much salt because it was making her puffy.

Then this wonderful spirit spoke about holding a tissue box for his daughter at her wedding as she is a bit of a crier, and how he thought the pearls were a beautiful added touch, along with her amazing song lineup.

Kathleen instantly said this was her dad. She confirmed he passed away from cancer in multiple organs and that he opted out of surgery because he believed wouldn't have made it through the holidays. She then confirmed that June was his birthday, the 11th was the day his nephew was born, December was all about his last Christmas, and January was the month he passed away.

Kathleen continued by letting me know that both her dad and her brother collected baseball cards and thought it was so sweet of her dad to make sure he spoke about her brother.

However, when she shared that she was getting married this month and how happy she was to know that not only did her dad know about her wedding, she couldn't believe how he knew about all the preparations—like adding the pearls to her dress and how she added Elvis's songs to the lineup to make sure it was a part of her wedding since they were both big Elvis fans. But it was his salt comment that not only called her out, it also made her promise to cut down on the salt, as she certainly didn't want to be puffy at her wedding. She was thankful to know that he was going to be there holding her tissues.

Heather Receives Nana's Warning

During this session, Heather's Nana came forward with a very direct warning. She spoke of Black Widow spiders in her boots that pinched her toes, warning her not to wear them without checking for the spiders first. Heather confirmed that in the NYC apartment where these boots were stored, they found Black Widow spiders in the closet.

zena

I'm Still Here

A young mom spirit came forward letting me know she recently passed away after a short battle with cancer of the pancreas. She immediately let me know she was under hospice care at the time of her passing with her family surrounding her. Then she spoke about her concern for her children who she left behind and showed me a boy and a girl and said, "I'm worried she's so angry and I want her to be okay."

Then I began to smell the scent of vanilla and she showed me a large round white candle with 3 wicks inside a white and gray bowl burning next to a window and said, "Tell her I'm still here, I'm still here."

This mom then focused on her son and said, "He's the quiet one, so I'm worried about him too. He's not going to school, tell him he's smart, so smart."

She continued, "I love them so much. I want them to know I am watching over them. Tell them I left it in the purple box."

When I asked her to provide more information about the purple box, she just repeated herself saying, "Tell them it is the purple box."

Since it appeared she didn't want to give me any additional information about the box, I moved on and asked her to provide me with something specific so her loved ones would know it was her talking. She showed me hard butterscotch candies and said, "It helped with the sickness."

She then said the month of March was significant, along with the numbers 12, 15, and 21.

Not a moment went by before Jennifer said this was her sister who passed away on March 21st from pancreatic cancer. She confirmed that her battle was over quickly and that she passed receiving hospice care while her family was with her.

Jennifer then confirmed she left behind two children, a 12-year-old boy and a 15-year-old girl. She also let me know that her daughter recently got into trouble at school and was fighting with everyone. Then she confirmed her son was also having a difficult time in school because he was not doing his work and skipping classes. Jennifer was shocked that her sister knew this was going on because when her sister was alive her children were so well-behaved and never got into trouble at school.

Before the session was over, Jennifer confirmed her sister's daughter had recently purchased a large round vanilla candle with 3 wicks in a white and gray ceramic bowl that she placed next to her bed by the window.

Jennifer was happy to learn that her sister was watching over them and said, "I can't wait to tell them their mom is still with them."

However, she had no idea what her sister was talking

about with the purple box but said she would ask the kids and let me know.

The next day I received an email that said, "It was a box on the shelf in her closet that they thought had just random things in it. However, when they opened it, they found that their mom put together a keepsake box full of all sorts of memory mementos and a personal letter she wrote to each of her children. They were so happy to find out about this box. Each read their letter right away and let me know that their mom left them advice for everything she will be missing as they grow up. Thank you for letting me know about the box. I just know this will make all the difference in the world."

CHAPTER 9

Children's Connections Across the Veil

CHILDREN WHO HAVE CROSSED over often recount experiences characterized by an intense sense of peace, warmth, and unconditional love. They describe encounters with benevolent beings, such as deceased loved ones, angels, spiritual guides, and the divine who embrace them with boundless compassion upon their arrival. Immediately, they are shown that love is a transformative force that tethers them to those left behind, not just an emotion. This understanding brings them comfort, knowing they are still connected to their loved ones.

These young people often gain profound insights into the nature of their own life experiences, transcending their tender years. Their recollections are often detailed regardless of their age at the time they ascended, and they express a deep understanding that their essence is no longer confined to their physical bodies, allowing them to be everywhere at once.

Some children report glimpses into future events, displaying a level of foresight that defies conventional explanation. They also share experiences and knowledge about the events of their passing and events they could have only witnessed after their passing. These insights display their ability to be present in spirit just moments after death.

However, many children who have crossed over often struggle to connect to their loved ones, as their messages are often misunderstood. Unfortunately, many loved ones do not comprehend or accept such phenomena, and this can lead to feelings of confusion for a child who has ascended but is still connected.

As their shift in perspective continues to expand in their new reality, it can disrupt the child's sense of normalcy making it even more difficult for those left behind to receive and understand their messages. As a result, many parents grapple to understand the transcendent nature of their child's spiritual essence.

The children's stories I have selected to share with you not only provide a compelling window into these insights and their innocence, but offer nothing less than awe-inspiring recollections, encounters, and vivid imagery. These connections provide a rich understanding of a child's transcendent experience. Through their communication, we see their boundless connections.

A Child Lost at Five

This connection started off with a sweet, energetic little boy coming forward talking about the month of June and the number 5. However, it didn't take long for this beautiful child to show me images and sounds of fire engines, while letting me know he passed because he couldn't breathe, showing me how the fluid filled his lungs, letting me know he drowned. To my surprise, right after he spoke about his passing, the connection took a happy turn, and this adorable little boy began running around yelling, "Paw Patrol, Paw Patrol!"

He then brought forward his three grandmas and a baby who did not take a breath in this life journey. He allowed me to see who he was with, shared that he was the one who would move and hide objects in his family, and told me through his giggles, "This is my favorite game to play."

Before I connected with his loved one, he made sure to let me know how much he was worried about his mom and needed to get a message to her that he loved her and was okay.

For Australian Elisha, that was it. Although she started to shake and cry, she quickly found the words to let me know that this was her 5-year-old nephew who had passed from a drowning accident that occurred on June 5th. She went on to confirm that soon after the ambulance arrived, the fire engines came for him. But for her, it was the running around yelling Paw Patrol that confirmed this was her nephew. Elisha shared that he loved these characters so much that he dressed up as them for Halloween and would run around yelling "Paw Patrol" when the show was about to start, just like I described.

Elisha then acknowledged she unknowingly blamed her toddler for the missing and moving objects but was happy to hear it was her nephew all along. She was thrilled to learn that he was visiting her and her family and said she should have known, as he was quite a cheeky little boy.

As the connection continued and Elisha heard the details from her nephew, her emotions deepened. She confirmed that the miscarriage he spoke about was her child and that she was overjoyed with happiness to know they were both with her grandma who passed one year after her nephew's accident, her great grandma, and his grandma from his maternal side.

Elisha understood that her nephew had come forward to not only let her know he was okay and with her unborn child, but he wanted to make sure his mom, who was struggling to cope with his passing, received his message about how much he loved her and that he was okay.

A Voice for Mia

During this connection an infant came forward letting me know she was born sick and had injured her head in her mommy's tummy. She was grateful to her mom who held her close in her white outfit and gave her the chance to say goodbye to everyone. She also spoke about the significance of June and the number 17.

After the details were shared, it was clear to one mother this was her daughter, Mia. Mia was diagnosed with cerebral fluid on her brain in utero and the doctors recommended an abortion. Despite this recommendation, Mia's mother chose to carry her daughter to term. At her birth, her mother confirmed she held Mia in her arms wearing a white outfit as everyone said their goodbyes. Mia passed on June 17.

Forever 16 Months Old

At the start of this session, a very young spirit came forward to connect with her mommy, saying she was 16. She immediately talked about a car accident that took her away and explained that her head was why she had to leave. She then began to show me a ring with a blue stone in it and started to kick her feet, asking me if I liked her new shoes.

Just as I finished my last word, Summer immediately confirmed she had lost her 16-month-old in a car accident from a head injury. Summer went on to explain that just before the accident occurred her husband had taken their daughter shopping, where he brought her new shoes and a new ring. Summer then confirmed the blue stone in the ring was her daughter's birthstone.

This connection was healing for both Summer and her beautiful daughter, who wanted to tell her mommy that she was okay but missed her very much.

Trickster Forever

As I began to connect to this spirit, something felt off. The energy was of a young child, but the spirit said they were a young adult who passed away from brain cancer after suffering from headaches, loss of balance, and vision issues. She let me know her battle was not long, and she liked to wrap herself in a white down comforter to comfort herself. Then this beautiful playful spirit showed me the pink, blue, and yellow Care Bears and let me know she was under hospice care with her family at the time of her passing. She also spoke about being a bit of a trickster by whispering in her loved one's left ear and that the month of April was significant to her.

Although I was confused by this ageless spirit I went forward with the information to watch how the story would unfold. Within a moment, Shan reached out and said this was her cousin who passed away from brain cancer at the age of seven but would now be 26.

Shan quickly confirmed all the information, including her cousin wrapping herself in a white down comforter for comfort and how they would play with the Care Bears all the time, especially the yellow one. She then confirmed her cousin's birthday was in April and how her left ear gets a funny feeling in it every time she gets anxious.

However, even though I knew this was the right connection, I was still confused by why this child spirit said she was a young adult. Then Shan filled in the missing piece. She let me know that the family keeps her living age by celebrating her birthday every year.

Once I heard that, I immediately understood why her cousin came forward not as the child she is, but at the age her family celebrates her. All I could think of at the time was what a brilliant child this was. To come forward in this way was to ensure her connection was made.

Squeezy Hugs for Everyone

A little girl spirit came forward with the cutest giggle. No matter what she talked about, it was always through laughter. Immediately she said, "I had a lung infection, so one day I stopped breathing and came here."

She then let me know her mom and dad were with her before she left, but she wasn't afraid to leave because, "I just knew everything would be okay."

Then this adorable little spirit told me how much she loved her birthday cupcakes with the frosting so high that when you bit into it, you would get it in your hair, and the soft-centered fruit candies that her grandma always gave her, giving her a few extra when mom wasn't looking.

However, my favorite part of this connection was when this little girl talked about how she still gives her mom and dad squeezy hugs and how they were the best in the world.

Joanne let me know that this was her daughter who passed away at the age of 5 from pneumonia. She confirmed that she and her husband were right by her side when their little girl took her last breath.

Then Joanne let me know about the story behind her daughter's cupcakes for her 5th birthday. After they brought them home, she left them on the kitchen counter and her little girl snuck into the kitchen to grab one and ate it. When her mom unexpectedly came back to the kitchen, her daughter tried to say she didn't take one, but the icing in her hair gave it away.

Joanne also confirmed that her mother-in-law would always have hard candies with soft fruit filling inside and was so glad that she let her daughter have a few extra when her grandma came to visit.

However, when her daughter spoke about the squeezy hugs, Joanne could no longer hold back her tears. She let me know that her daughter would run up to everyone in the family and give the best squeezy hugs. "She hugged everyone like it was the last hug she would ever give."

Joanne was so happy to know her beautiful daughter was still giggling as she always did and that the tingling and warmth through her body was her little girl giving her squeezy hugs.

No More Squishy Face

An adorable little girl came forward and told me she didn't have any more pain in her head and that her "squishy face was gone."

Then she couldn't stop talking about playing with Beanie Babies and showed me how she loved to sing while spinning around and around, making me a bit nauseous as I watched her spin.

She was so proud to show me how she could spin again and said, "Now I can spin, before I left, I couldn't even walk."

At that point, this wonderful spirit spoke about painted rocks and how beautiful they were, letting me know, "These were the ones I painted with mommy."

Then she let me know that the months of April, May, and June were significant to her, along with the number 3.

Kelly immediately knew this was her 3-year-old niece who had a large cancerous tumor on her face, which she confirmed her niece called "squishy face." She then confirmed April was when her niece's eye became black. In May it had grown and by June they found out it was cancer. After that Kelly let me know that the cancer spread throughout her body, and they stopped counting at twenty tumors.

Then Kelly confirmed her niece's love of Beanie Babies and how they always played with them together, and her love of spinning, which by the end of her life was taken away because she could no longer walk.

At the end of the connection, Kelly let me know the rocks that her niece and her mother painted were all around her grave, and Kelly was so happy to learn her niece knew they were there.

your loved ones are always with you

Chasing Butterflies

A young boy came forward and said he was in a car and had an accident, but not a car accident. Then he let me know it had to do with his head, but not a head injury. I was very confused by this little boy, however, he said, "My mom will know what happened."

At that point, I left that information alone and asked him what else he wanted to share with me. That is when he talked about his pants falling at school, his love of his sneakers, and holding his mom's hand.

Then he said, "I have one more thing to share. Tell my mom I'm still chasing the butterflies."

Not truly understanding the meaning behind most of these messages, I revealed the information as I received it, knowing his mom would understand. Within a minute, Marina knew this was her son who passed away at age 7 in the back seat of the car when he choked on a toy.

Once Marina told the story about how he passed it all began to make sense. I now completely understood why her son was describing his passing the way he did.

Then Marina confirmed that his pants fell at school and that he was very affectionate, always holding her hand. However, when she let me know about the sneakers, she said, "I have his sneakers and smell them sometimes, as they still smell like him."

Marina finished the connection by letting me know, "He was always chasing butterflies and now they are always at the cemetery."

CHAPTER 10

The Eternal Journey of Unborn Souls

IN THE REALM BEYOND our physical existence, where time and space hold little sway, the journey of souls begins long before they take their first breath. Among these souls are the ones who depart this world before they even have a chance to experience life outside the womb. I will tread lightly in this chapter, as we explore this tender topic that arouses a whirlwind of emotions within the hearts of those touched by such profound loss.

The spirit of an unborn or stillborn baby begins its extraordinary journey of transcendence where its physical life encounters its untimely end, and the spirit of the unborn child emerges from the confines of its earthly dwelling. This transition is marked by a gentle release from the physical realm to the awaiting angelic hands ready to cradle their essence. These souls are met with an outpouring of compassion for their interrupted journey and the void that echoes through the hearts of their earthly parents.

While the circumstances surrounding the departure of these souls may differ, their ultimate destiny remains unchanged: a spiritual evolution that surpasses human understanding. They are enveloped in a blanket of unconditional love, where pain is soothed, wounds are mended, and their essence is nurtured.

This love permeates every facet of their existence. Unborn souls are surrounded by angelic beings whose purpose is to guide, heal, and support these precious spirits. They offer comfort, understanding, and reassurance as the souls acclimate to their newfound state of being.

One might wonder, what becomes of these unborn souls? Do they forever yearn for the life they were denied? The truth is comforting to those who have walked in these shoes.

The unborn or stillborn spirit, although not having lived a life as we know it, still carries its own purpose. Each soul has a chosen path, and sometimes the briefest of encounters on this earthly plane holds the most profound significance. Their time here, however fleeting, has the power to transform and shape the lives of those they touch.

In the spiritual realm, these souls engage in a process of self-discovery and evolution. They connect with other souls who have undergone similar experiences for support and understanding. These souls hold no grudges or resentments, for they possess an awareness that their journey serves a higher purpose. Through their existence, no matter how brief, they understand they have imparted a deep well of love that ripples through time and eternity.

While the loss of an unborn life is undoubtedly a source of immeasurable pain and grief, the journey of these precious souls transcends the realm of sorrow. These beautiful spirits become beacons of light for their earthly parents, guiding them along their own journey of healing and self-discovery. In the depths of grief and loss, a connection is formed—an eternal bond that transcends the limitations of physical existence. The spirits of these unborn children continue to walk alongside their parents, offering comfort, strength, and a reminder that love knows no boundaries.

In the earthly realm, the bond between the unborn soul and its parents remains unbroken. Love endures, transcending the boundaries of life and death. This connection continues to exist, allowing the parents to draw strength from the eternal bond they share with their children. Through dreams, signs, and moments of serendipity, the spirit of the unborn reaches out, assuring its parents of their presence.

As time unfolds, the unborn souls partake in a variety of lessons tailored to their individual journeys. Some may choose to act as spirit guides for their grieving parents, while others immerse themselves in the study of compassion, cultivating an understanding that transcends physical existence.

However, in some cases the spirit may choose to reincarnate, returning to Earth to fulfill its unfinished purpose or to take on a new adventure. In these instances, the spirit carefully selects the circumstances of its new life, seeking opportunities for growth, love, and the realization of its divine essence. This decision is made with the utmost care, guided by the wisdom and love that has blossomed within, along with divine angelic guidance.

I chose to share the following connection in hopes of providing an understanding of the light these unborn souls bring to our world.

Message From a Lost Daughter

During this beautiful connection, an infant daughter came forward to connect to her mom who blamed herself for her stillbirth. The daughter immediately spoke about January 27th and the number 88. As the daughter continued, she let me know she had a specific message for her mom. The message was clear: "Don't put the silver frame away."

Within a moment her mom came forward and confirmed her birthday was January 27th and her daughter's due date was August 8th. However, at the time of this connection, the mom didn't understand why her stillborn daughter would give her the message about the picture frame she had purchased for her daughter's first photo. Although, one year later, it became clear. The mother sent me an email letting me know she had just given birth to a beautiful baby girl and the picture frame she had purchased a year earlier now held the image of her newborn baby girl.

CHAPTER 11

The Journey of Our Departed Pets

AS PET OWNERS, WE share a unique and deep bond with our animal companions. They bring joy, love, and unwavering loyalty into our lives. Unfortunately, when the inevitable moment arrives, we must bid farewell to our beloved friends. The loss of a cherished pet can be heart-wrenching, leaving us with a profound sense of grief and longing. In our search for solace and understanding, many of us find ourselves pondering the question: What happens to our departed pets when they die?

When our pets pass away, they begin a similar journey of peace and happiness in the eternal realm. Our departed companions are restored to perfect health and vitality, reuniting with our beloved loved ones and other pets they may have known or interacted with during their time on Earth.

Through my connections with many departed pets, I have learned that they continue watching over us from realms beyond the veil. Some become spirit guides and guardians, while others are there to bring us comfort and healing through subtle signs, dreams, or unexplained sensations.

As we navigate the sorrow of losing our pets, let us hold onto the cherished memories, the love, and the joy they brought into our lives. While we may long for their physical presence, their spirits remain with us, forever intertwined in the layers of our hearts.

Within the spiritual realm, pet spirits are guided by a unique set of motivations, frequently coming forward to communicate with the loved ones they left behind, creating a bridge over the veil. These motivations are rooted in the enduring love and unique connections forged during their time on Earth.

As we explore the realm of pet spirit communication, we gain insights into the timeless nature of these bonds. We find comfort in the knowledge that the spirits of our cherished animal companions continue to weave their presence into the fabric of our daily lives through messages centered around several themes.

The first and most common theme is unconditional love knows no bounds. This profound bond between humans and their pets is marked by an unconditional love that extends beyond the physical realm. Pet spirits are drawn to their owners by this enduring love, seeking to convey a sense of continued companionship and reassurance. They choose to revisit their owners to contribute to the growth and evolution of both the pet's soul and the human spirit. These encounters become integral chapters in their shared spiritual stories.

For those pets who have spent their lives being our caretakers, the theme of guardianship from beyond is found in their hearts and communications. These pet spirits take on a protective role from the spiritual realm. They watch over their owners, offering comfort and protection during times of distress. Their ethereal presence becomes a source of support and a reminder that the connection forged in life persists in the afterlife.

However, for pets who have been our healers, their connection is of healing energy. As their energy in life held a unique capacity for healing, their spirit continues to bring this comfort during times of grief, using their ethereal essence to soothe the hearts of their grieving owners. The warmth of their love persists, offering relief to their owner's time of healing from their loss.

Sometimes, the next theme is discounted by those with disbelief. Yet, for those who believe, many of our pets will communicate through symbolic messages and signs. Whether we hear a familiar bark, a gentle purr, or feel the subtle sensation of a phantom tail brushing against a leg, these symbolic gestures from our pets serve as a means of reaching out. These gestures allow their presence to be known in a language that transcends the spoken word.

I have selected the following stories to shed light on the profound connections that are possible between our beloved pets and their owners.

# Ozzy Bear

During this fur baby connection, a very special dog named Ozzy came forward. He was Ashley's best friend and companion. She had him longer than she had been married, and longer than her kids had been alive. This beautiful spirit was there for her highs and lows, the good and the bad, her wedding planning, and the birth of her children. Ozzy was her first baby as an adult and truly her best friend.

As the session began, Ozzy immediately came through and described their last moments together. He showed me how Ashley brought his paws to her face and kissed them at home, while she said how sorry she was for what was about to take place. He shared with me how much pain he was in because of being attacked by another dog and in that moment, he wanted her to know he understood what she was doing and was saying "Thank you" as she said, "I'm sorry."

A moment later, Ozzy described the long seat he was placed on when going to the vet. Ashley confirmed their truck has a front bench seat and her husband has a song he plays that makes him think of Ozzy called "Bench Seat."

your loved ones are always with you

Then Ozzy continued and spoke about the moment her husband was with him at the vet and how he stood next to him while petting his head. All of which her husband confirmed.

I explained to Ashley how her beautiful fur baby wanted her to know that he was okay with her decision, and how he took in each of their last moments together before he said his final goodbye.

Ozzy then let Ashley know how he is still present in her days. He described a dog bed in front of the couch on the left where he currently visits. Ashley explained to me that this dog bed had only been there for the past few months, months after he had passed.

Ozzy continued by showing me how he was snapping at the bugs on a camping river rafting trip, which Ashley shared was one of her favorite memories with Ozzy. She also confirmed that the life vest that Ozzy wore was blue-and-green striped, just as I described to her.

I then shared with Ashley how special his calm, peaceful, and quiet energy was during the connection. I explained to her how this meant he was at peace and so very happy to see that she brought a new puppy into her life to continue her healing process.

Ashley then shared with me how quiet it was when he left, despite having two kids, two dogs, and a husband who were all very loud—her home was quiet. However, it wasn't until this connection that Ashley realized this quiet wasn't sadness, it was peace. It was Ozzy's way of telling her he was at peace, the storm had calmed, and the world hadn't crashed down.

Ashley now understood the meaning behind the calm, peaceful stillness.

At the end of the session, I looked back at the images he sent at the beginning of the session, and I knew these images were revealed to bring healing to Ashley. The first image was a bear with the message of "home" and the second was of an eagle signifying "spirit has my back." To my surprise, Ashley turned around and revealed a large, wonderful tattoo of a bear on her back and couldn't believe the confirmation she just received.

It's My Tongue, Mommy

This beautiful fur baby spirit came through right away. He was excited to be there, and his emotions came through so strongly that they even brought tears to my eyes. This sweet, adorable dog named Charlie immediately connected to his owner and said she was the best mommy. One of the sweetest parts of the connection for me was how Charlie would refer to his owner as mommy and mama throughout the entire session.

As he came forward, I was able to describe his face, and he brought my attention to his tongue sticking out of his mouth as a distinct feature—as if this would make sure his mommy knew it was him. Then he began to talk about the square meat he was given and how much he loved it. He went on to say how he now comes into the kitchen while his mommy is cooking, and that she always gives the other two dogs food but always forgets him. He told me he holds the space between the two dogs and to please not forget him next time. Then he showed me an image of an emerald green flannel shirt, on which he was sitting.

As Charlie continued, he spoke about being in a lot of pain during his last days and wanted to reassure his mommy that she did the right thing by helping him leave. As he continued to talk about their last moments together, I could feel his love for his mommy. He referred to how she kissed his right paw in the spot where it hurt and that he was very thankful for the words she whispered in his ear as he passed because it made him feel so loved.

The last message Charlie gave before we ended the connection, was an image of twisted fabric with frayed ends, and said to his mommy, "Please don't throw it away because it's my favorite toy."

Diana immediately confirmed this was her Charlie who had stage 3 renal failure at the end of his life. She shared that the description of his face and the very distinct feature of his tongue sticking out was all she needed to hear to know that this was her Charlie. She then shared that he had lost most of his teeth due to old age, which is why his tongue hung out of his mouth.

Moments later, Diana then laughed as I used my hand to create a square in the air to describe his meat and shared, "Because of not having his teeth, we couldn't feed him regular food and had to buy him wet food that came in small square trays. The food inside looked like chunks of meat."

Diana then continued to confirm the flannel shirt and said, "The only flannel I own is emerald green, I'll show it to you."

The minute she brought it forward I knew it was the exact emerald green plaid shirt Charlie had shown me.

Diana then confirmed that Charlie always laid on the clothes she would leave on the ground in the bathroom.

Diana then recognized the twisted fabric with frayed ends as his favorite toy, but she said, "Oh honey, I threw that away a long time ago."

Charlie quickly replied, "No mama, it's in the house."

After the session, she did find his favorite toy, just as described —a rope with frayed ends. It was in a toy box that was put away in a closet.

Diana then confirmed how difficult his passing was and how much pain he was in during those last days and was so glad to be reassured that she did the right thing by calling the vet to help him let go. Diana shared that she never had to put a pet down, so the thought of setting an appointment just for that was something she couldn't wrap her head around. She even took time off from work and would carry him outside and they would listen to music under her apple tree, in hopes he would pass on his own. Unfortunately, he hung on.

However, on his last day, she shared with me that she heard him whimper and that was when she called a 24-hour vet to her home and knew it was time. She then confirmed that she had kissed his right paw where they put in the IV and had whispered in his ear when he passed. She was so thankful to know he heard what she said and that it made him feel loved.

Diana then explained that because her home is bilingual all her kids call her mommy and mama and couldn't believe he did too. Before we ended the session she asked if he knew about the tattoo she was going to get of him.

He said, "You don't have to do that mama, I'm with you always, I'm in your heart. You are beautiful just the way you are."

Saint Bernard Protection

Five months and two days after Katie's beloved Saint Bernard, Beauregard, passed from hemangiosarcoma, a cancer of the spleen, she came to me to connect with his spirit. Beauregard, also adoringly known as Beau, Biggy, and my personal favorite, Stromboli, shared a decade of life with Katie.

At the start of the connection, I asked Katie if he had any special markings since he was one of many Saint Bernards waiting from beyond the veil. She let me know that he had the sweetest arrangement of freckles on his face, which she called his constellation freckles.

Not a moment later, he came forward and immediately highlighted his left cheek, showing off his freckles to me, and I shared this with Katie.

She took a moment, then replied, "Yes, on the left side."

Despite the overflowing tears and the lump in her throat, she seemed relieved to know he was here. As I continued, I spoke calmly and clearly, ensuring she understood each message that he came forward to share with her. He told her he was okay and that he understood why she had to make the final decision to let him go.

Katie silently shook her head in agreement, as her beloved Saint Barnard continued to show me how they laid face-to-face together on the floor during his final days. After sharing this with Katie, she immediately closed her eyes and confirmed that during the last three days, leading up to his passing, she was laying on the floor with him, stroking his face to help calm his cries so he could rest, despite his pain.

As her sweet Beau continued, I let Katie know that he was telling me how she wished she would have known sooner how sick he was. However, he also shared with me that there was no way she could have known—this was quick, it moved fast and started in his intestines.

Katie then confirmed how she blames herself for not knowing how sick he was, despite knowing that he struggled with gut health, which started about a year before his passing. She shared that he narrowly survived bloat—a potentially fatal condition where his stomach twisted and decreased blood flow to his vital organs.

"Luckily," Katie said, "he survived the surgery without sustaining damage."

Unfortunately, the moment Katie shared this her beloved Saint Barnard said, "No, there was existing damage to my intestines prior to the surgery."

He then showed me what looked like ulcers and Katie let me know that this was correct, sharing with me that he did have a very sensitive stomach and was being treated for acid reflux prior to this emergency surgery.

I then let Katie know how grateful he was to her for having found him. She shared with me that she got her family on board with getting another Saint Bernard under the condition he would be for her dad for Father's Day. Long story short, when she went to see the puppies, she locked eyes with the smallest one in the litter, and that sweet pipsqueak, Beau, would be hers from that moment on.

I let her know that her beloved Beauregard felt the same connection in the same moment and confirmed they were truly soul-bound.

Katie then expressed to me that when she lost him it felt like she had lost a son and wondered if he would come back to her in this life journey. I then repeated the words of her beloved. He expressed how they shared a special bond, and he would make sure she had everything she needed.

I then smiled and told her the wonderful news that when he passed, he signed on to be her animal spirit guide, guiding and protecting her through this lifetime.

As we wrapped up the session, Katie asked who he was with and I let her know there were two older women and one younger woman with him, which she confirmed as her MawMaw, MomMom, and her Aunt Diane.

Katie then asked, "Who received Beau when he passed?"

I responded, "There's an older gentleman here saying he was with him at the time of passing."

Katie immediately smiled and said, "My PawPaw."

Katie was at peace knowing he was received by the man who first showed her how beautiful the bond between a person and a Saint could be.

The session was moments from ending before Katie peered down at the mementos she brought to honor Beauregard's spirit. At that point, she raised her oracle card to show me and said, "Vervain Everlasting. I'd pull this card every time I practiced readings with Beauregard. It says, 'Spellbound. Soul alignment. Release. Protection.' Every word affirms this connection. Thank you."

Hush Puppy Nacho

Susana came to me to connect to her beautiful basset hound named Nacho. The session began with Nacho identifying himself by what I thought were his final moments at the vet clinic, by insisting his left side was hurting, over his shoulder onto his back.

This confused Susana at first until she remembered Nacho's surgery, where he had a tumor that grew into his shoulder and the doctors had to take quite a lot of mass from his left side because it seeped into the muscle. The surgery was a few months before his passing, which is why it provoked confusion. However, I explained to Susana it was just his way of bringing something forward that she would quickly understand, so she would know it was him.

Nacho then describes his right paw and arm being numb, which is where his IV had been administered. Now Susana was sure it was him because Nacho was in the vet clinic when he passed away. Unfortunately, he had been in and out of the clinic over the past year due to a tick bite he received during one of his walks in the park. From that point forward, his health started to decline.

Nacho let me know this time he was very sick and was not even able to eat. He spoke about being in the kennel for a few days until he laid down on his left side and passed away. Susana confirmed this is how she found him when she got to the clinic.

He quickly reassured Susana that he did not suffer and that his passing was quick. Susana again confirmed that she was told by the vet that his blood pressure suddenly dropped, and he went quickly. At just twelve years old he now lays to rest on her mantel at home.

Susana's main question for the session is whether Nacho resented the fact that she and her sister hadn't been able to be with him when he passed. Nacho immediately replied that he wasn't and waited for them before he ascended, as he knew they were coming. He then described how, when they got to the clinic, Susana lifted his ear and whispered something into it, letting me know he heard every word she said.

Susana was overwhelmed, even though those moments were hard for her to look back on, and confirmed lifting his ear and telling him how much she loved him and that he could rest now.

At this point, Susana shared with me that Nacho had very big, floppy ears, and during playtime, she'd wiggle his ears until he barked at her, as if she was pulling at them. Of course, she wasn't.

She said, "He would just overreact over everything to do with his ears. Nacho saying that I had lifted his ear, along with the motion of your arm fully raised as he indicated, now amuses me, since everything to do with his ears was highly exaggerated."

Nacho shared that Susana stayed with him for a while, petting his ear just as he used to like it. Then he described who was in the room with him, saying there was a man and two more women. Susana confirmed this was true, as she and her sister were there, along with the male doctor and a female doctor whose shift was over but had stayed to offer them their condolences and to say goodbye to Nacho.

Nacho proceeded to describe his bed at home, showing a fluffy beige kind of pillow. Susana quickly said, "This was not his bed, but the living room couch he took over. Since he had short legs, he would jump on it with his two front paws and bark at us so that we would help him onto it. We would oblige and hoist him onto the couch, which then became a habit of his."

Nacho proudly claimed this as his bed and told me he still likes sleeping there.

Susana let me know that she would not have it any other way, the couch is his.

Nacho confirmed that he visits Susana quite often and typically stays on her right side with his head on her lap. Susana let me know that she wasn't surprised by this as she got Nacho tattooed on her right arm a month after his passing and was glad to learn he still comes around.

She even shared with me that her sister can sometimes feel him brush up against her when she's in the kitchen, just like he used to do. And Susana, from time to time, can hear his wagging tail hitting the table legs in the living room. This was the confirmation she needed to know it was all him.

By the end of the session, Susana let me know it was difficult to come up with questions as she was already overwhelmed and said, "Even though I had never had a two-way conversation with Nacho, the answers are very 'Nacho-like.'"

Susana continued and said, "I know I'm talking to him. Your whole demeanor, the way you imitate him, the way he describes things, I can even see him answering your questions just like that."

At that point, all she wanted to know was if he was happy with them.

Nacho immediately showed me an image of himself walking in between someone's legs and telling me this was his life and he had been so very happy.

Susana smiled and said, "I'd stand over Nacho and hug him between my legs and walk around with him like this. It fills me with so much warmth, joy, and relief to know that he was happy."

CHAPTER 12

Barriers to Connection Across the Veil

ALTHOUGH THERE ARE PEOPLE born with the ease of experiencing a quiet or still place through which connections with the dead are almost second nature, most people must work to achieve this ability—like any other skill. So, can anyone learn this to connect to those who have crossed over the veil? With work and perseverance, the answer is "yes."

However, the ability to connect with departed loved ones is often hindered by various factors involving the emotional, psychological, and spiritual realms. Despite the presence of subtle messages, the living may not recognize or interpret them for several reasons. Understanding these obstacles provides insights into the challenges the living face when seeking to connect to their beloved across the veil.

One key barrier to receiving messages from our beloved seems to be the intensity of the grief felt by those left behind. This emotion, combined with loss and sorrow, can create a wall of anguish that hinders the ability to receive spiritual messages. This overwhelming pain blocks subtle signals and energies from the other side meant to bring comfort and connection.

Skepticism and disbelief can also pose a hindrance to those wanting reassurance that their loved ones are still with them. These individuals approach spiritual experiences with a skeptical mindset and formulate doubt due to the lack of empirical evidence. This skepticism, founded in the need for tangible proof, creates an ongoing barrier for the living to receive messages that may be sent by the departed.

Fear is another barrier faced by loved ones looking to make these connections. The fear of confronting the emotional pain associated with their loss and the fear of the unknown can create a defense mechanism that blocks the flow of spiritual energy. Only through the elimination of these fears, and having the willingness to open one's heart and mind, can a connection beyond the physical world be made.

Daily life with the hustle and bustle of everyday existence, coupled with the demands of work and family, can also leave little room for quiet and reflective time. The noise of the physical world simply drowns out the whispers from the spiritual realm, especially when the messages are subtle or difficult to recognize, and we don't know the cues to pay attention to.

Some individuals expect dramatic or preconceived signs and overlook the simple, quiet signs that their beloved ones have sent. It is often the simple signs of symbolic gestures, synchronicities, or seemingly ordinary occurrences that the living is blind to receiving. Recognizing these subtleties requires an openness to interpreting the world beyond its surface meanings. The mismatch between grand expectations and ordinary messages, combined with the lack of awareness from those left behind, leads to the dismissal of many communications.

At times, cultural and societal influences can also play a significant role in how easily one can miss connections to the other side. Barriers can be created by cultural or religious beliefs that foster skepticism or make these types of communications taboo. These beliefs often skew perceptions, creating psychological roadblocks that prevent any type of communication across the veil. Overcoming this barrier takes a multifaceted approach to dealing with the external pressures and internal limitations created by the boundaries set in place by these structures.

Through grief counseling, spiritual practices, seeking help from mediums, and becoming mindful throughout their daily lives, many can expand their awareness to identify the signs and symbols of messages from their beloved. There are also several practices that can strengthen your ability to receive messages between the realms.

When the living wishes to connect to a departed loved one, the first requirement is to release any skepticism you may be harboring and embrace the possibility of spiritual communication. This open mindset creates a perfect environment for subtle messages to be recognized.

I also recommend allowing yourself time and space to grieve and heal. Since grief can act as a barrier to spiritual connections, using counseling, support groups, or personal reflection to support your emotional healing is vital to being able to open yourself up to spiritual energies.

Once you feel you are ready, create a quiet space, both externally and internally, where you feel calm and centered. This will aid spiritual experiences and increase your ability to practice mindfulness. These practices can increase your awareness, sharpen your intuition, and permit the receipt of subtle signs.

These signs can come in the form of meaningful coincidences or patterns that catch your attention throughout your daily life. These signals are the significant occurrences sent from your beloved.

You may also want to keep your dreams in mind, as they can serve as a bridge between the physical and spiritual realms. Many times, dreams will carry symbolic or direct messages from those across the veil.

As you grow in these practices, trust your instincts and intuitive feelings. Often, these subtle messages from your beloved are personal and unique experiences that come in the form of gut feelings, inner knowing, sudden insights, or signs. Be patient with yourself and allow your growth to unfold organically without judgment. Remain open to these spiritual connections as they strengthen the bonds between you and your beloved.

CHAPTER 13

Spirit Guides and Guardians: Nurturing Souls Beyond Death

THROUGHOUT OUR LIVES, THE concept of death often evokes fear, uncertainty, and sorrow. We view it as an ending, a cessation of our existence as we know it. Yet together, we have come to realize death is merely a transition—an opening to an extraordinary journey of the spirit guided by benevolent beings entrusted with our well-being.

By accepting that your journey transcends the limitations of this physical realm, you understand that your actions have consequences, not only in this lifetime but in the tapestry of your existence. With this knowledge, you become a conscious co-creator of your life. Shaping your destiny through the choices you make and the love you share.

Understanding this continuation of your essence beyond mortality has far-reaching implications. It invites you to reevaluate the purpose and meaning of your life. As you move forward to accept the inevitability of death, embrace the motivation to live authentically, pursue your passions, and cultivate meaningful connections with others. This will inspire you to savor each moment and seize the beauty of your life journey.

Interdependency is perhaps one of the most significant implications of comprehending the fate of the spirit. This fosters a deep sense of connection with yourself, with others, and with the world around you. Once you recognize the interdependence of all beings, you cultivate empathy, compassion, and reverence for life. Your understanding grows to accept that your spirit is intrinsically connected to the spirit within every living being and that your actions ripple through the collective consciousness—igniting a deep sense of responsibility to contribute to the well-being of those you encounter on your journey.

Keep in mind that living fully with the knowledge of the afterlife requires a balance between embracing the transcendent and remaining grounded in the present. We must not become so preoccupied with the mysteries of the beyond that we neglect the beauty of the here and now. Instead, I encourage you to integrate this understanding into your daily lives, infusing your interactions, choices, and pursuits with a sense of purpose and meaning.

In life, each soul has its own set of personal spirit guides and angels tailored to their unique needs and life path to help foster their life meaning. These guides are intimately connected to the individual, accompanying them throughout their life journey. The interaction between these benevolent beings and the souls is predominantly on the metaphysical level, through the language of intuition and signs.

During an individual's life, these beings actively participate in the growth and development of souls, acting as spiritual cheerleaders, offering encouragement and inspiration to navigate challenges, fostering resilience and perseverance, and applying detours when appropriate. These entities bring clarity during times of confusion, helping souls gain insight into their life lessons and karmic patterns. Through their presence, these guides empower souls to fulfill their highest purpose and manifest their innate potential.

Trusting the guidance of these guardians is essential for the soul's growth. While the physical world often prioritizes tangible evidence, the spiritual realm operates on a different plane of existence. Souls must learn to tune into their inner knowing, cultivating trust in the messages and signs provided by their guides. This trust serves as a foundation for the soul's continued expansion and deepening connection with its spiritual support system in the afterlife.

The nature of these spiritual connections is not random. Entities are assigned to souls with purpose. They share a sincere connection with the spirits they guide. Whether they are spirit guides, angels, or beloved ancestors, they serve as guardians guiding the soul. They possess an innate understanding of the life challenges faced by the souls they are assigned to and are uniquely equipped to assist in their transcendence when the time comes.

In life, as well as in death, the relationship between one's guides and the souls they accompany is not static. As souls progress and evolve, their guides may change to match their new levels of awareness and growth. Guides may step back, allowing the soul greater independence, or new guides may emerge to provide specialized guidance for specific aspects of the soul's journey. The relationships forged between souls and their guides are dynamic and fluid, adapting to the ever-changing needs of the spirit.

Their purpose extends beyond mere protection; they are the soul's compassionate mentors, wise teachers, and steadfast companions. These ethereal entities play a vital role in the soul's continued evolution towards its divine purpose. These spirit guides, angels, and beloved loved ones are truly the unseen allies of the soul's journey beyond death. With their understanding, unconditional love, and unwavering guidance, they empower souls to navigate the complexities of the afterlife, helping souls forge ahead seamlessly.

As we reach the final moments of our journey together, I want to remind you that death is not to be feared but accepted as a continuation of the soul's evolution beyond the confines of time and space. Allow this knowledge to inspire you to live each moment with intention and unlock the doors to spiritual growth, and deeper connections to your personal spiritual team, gain an appreciation for your existence, and embrace the connections you receive from your loved ones across the veil.

ZENA, a private intuitive and Clairsentient with over 20 years of experience in spiritual communication, has served as a trusted consultant to diverse individuals, including notable names in entertainment and business. Her intuitive journey, rooted in a childhood immersed in a generational spiritual gift, took a profound turn after a life-altering encounter with the angelic realm. Realizing her purpose, Zena became a Master Bereavement Consultant, dedicated to forging connections between individuals and their departed loved ones, animal companions, and spiritual guides. With a global perspective shaped by encounters with various cultures and religious leaders, Zena recently expanded her reach to TikTok, aiming to provide guidance and healing to a wider audience on their spiritual journeys.

tiktok.com/@angelwhisperzena

**MORE FROM
THOUGHT CATALOG BOOKS**

Ceremony
—*Brianna Wiest*

Dream Journal
—*Danica Gim*

Manifesting for Beginners: A Step By Step Guide To Attracting A Life You Love
—*Victoria Jackson*

Through The Veils of Mystery: Into The Depths, An Exploration Of Invisible Inner Realms
—*Kristina Bazan*

How You'll Do Everything Based On Your Zodiac Sign
—*Chrissy Stockton*

THOUGHT
CATALOG
Books

THOUGHTCATALOG.COM

THOUGHT
CATALOG
Books

Thought Catalog Books is a publishing imprint of Thought Catalog, a digital magazine for thoughtful storytelling, and is owned and operated by The Thought & Expression Co. Inc., an independent media group based in the United States of America. Founded in 2010, we are committed to helping people become better communicators and listeners to engender a more exciting, attentive, and imaginative world. The Thought Catalog Books imprint connects Thought Catalog's digital-native roots with our love of traditional book publishing. The books we publish are designed as beloved art pieces. We publish work we love. Pioneering an author-first and holistic approach to book publishing, Thought Catalog Books has created numerous best-selling print books, audiobooks, and eBooks that are being translated in over 30 languages.

ThoughtCatalog.com | **Thoughtful Storytelling**

ShopCatalog.com | **Shop Books + Curated Products**